The Spirit of Robbie Burns

Robert Murray

Other Books by Robert Murray

The Grocer's Boy:
A Slice of His Life in 1950s Scotland

THE SPIRIT OF ROBBIE BURNS

Robert Murray

The Spirit of Robbie Burns by Robert Murray.

First edition published in Great Britain in 2019 by Extremis Publishing Ltd., Suite 218, Castle House, 1 Baker Street, Stirling, FK8 1AL, United Kingdom.
www.extremispublishing.com

Extremis Publishing is a Private Limited Company registered in Scotland (SC509983) whose Registered Office is Suite 218, Castle House, 1 Baker Street, Stirling, FK8 1AL, United Kingdom.

Copyright © Robert Murray, 2019.

Robert Murray has asserted the moral right under the Copyright, Designs and Patents Act 1988 to be identified as the author of this work.

Applications for permission for any use whatsoever of all or any part of this work must be made in advance, before any such intended use. No performance may be given without the receipt of a licence from the author and publisher.

The views expressed in this work are solely those of the author, and do not necessarily reflect those of the publisher. The publisher hereby disclaims any responsibility for them.

This book is a work of non-fiction. Unless otherwise noted, the author and the publisher make no explicit guarantees as to the accuracy of the information included in this book.

This book may include references to organisations, feature films, television programmes, popular songs, musical bands, novels, reference books, and other creative works, the titles of which are trademarks and/or registered trademarks, and which are the intellectual properties of their respective copyright holders.

All rights reserved. No part of this publication may be reproduced, stored in a retrieval system, or transmitted, in any form or by any means, electronic, mechanical, photocopying, recording or otherwise, without the prior permission in writing of the publisher.

This book is sold subject to the condition that it shall not, by way of trade or otherwise, be lent, re-sold or hired out, or otherwise circulated without the publisher's prior consent in any form of binding or cover other than that in which it is published and without a similar condition including this condition being imposed on the subsequent purchaser.

A CIP catalogue record for this book is available from the British Library.

ISBN: 978-0-9955897-6-6

Typeset in Goudy Bookletter 1911, designed by The League of Moveable Type.
Printed and bound in Great Britain by IngramSpark, Chapter House, Pitfield, Kiln Farm, Milton Keynes, MK11 3LW, United Kingdom.

Front cover artwork is Copyright © Everett Historical at Shutterstock.
Back cover artwork by Armigru from Pixabay.
Incidental stock images sourced from Pixabay unless otherwise indicated.

Cover design and book design is Copyright © Thomas A. Christie.
Author images are Copyright © Eleanor Jewson.
The copyrights of third parties are reserved. All third party imagery is used under the provision of Fair Use for the purposes of commentary and criticism.
Internal photographic illustrations are sourced from the author's personal collection, unless otherwise indicated.

Contents

Preface .... Page 1
Introductory Notes .... Page 9

Stage Directions .... Page 13
Dramatis Personae .... Page 19

The Spirit of Robbie Burns
Part I: "Poverty in Ayrshire" .... Page 21
Part II: "High Society in Edinburgh" ..... Page 51
Part III: "Farming Life in Dumfries" ...... Page 71

Appendix I: Address to a Haggis .... Page 89
Appendix II: The Selkirk Grace .... Page 93
Appendix III: A Typical Burns Night Menu ... Page 95
Appendix IV: The Loyal Toast .... Page 97
Appendix V: The Immortal Memory (Example) ... Page 99
Appendix VI: Address to the Lassies (Example) ... Page 107
Appendix VII: Reply from the Lassies (Example) ... Page 111
Appendix VIII: Auld Lang Syne .... Page 113

Illustrations .... Page 115
Acknowledgements .... Page 129
About the Author .... Page 131

Map of Scotland

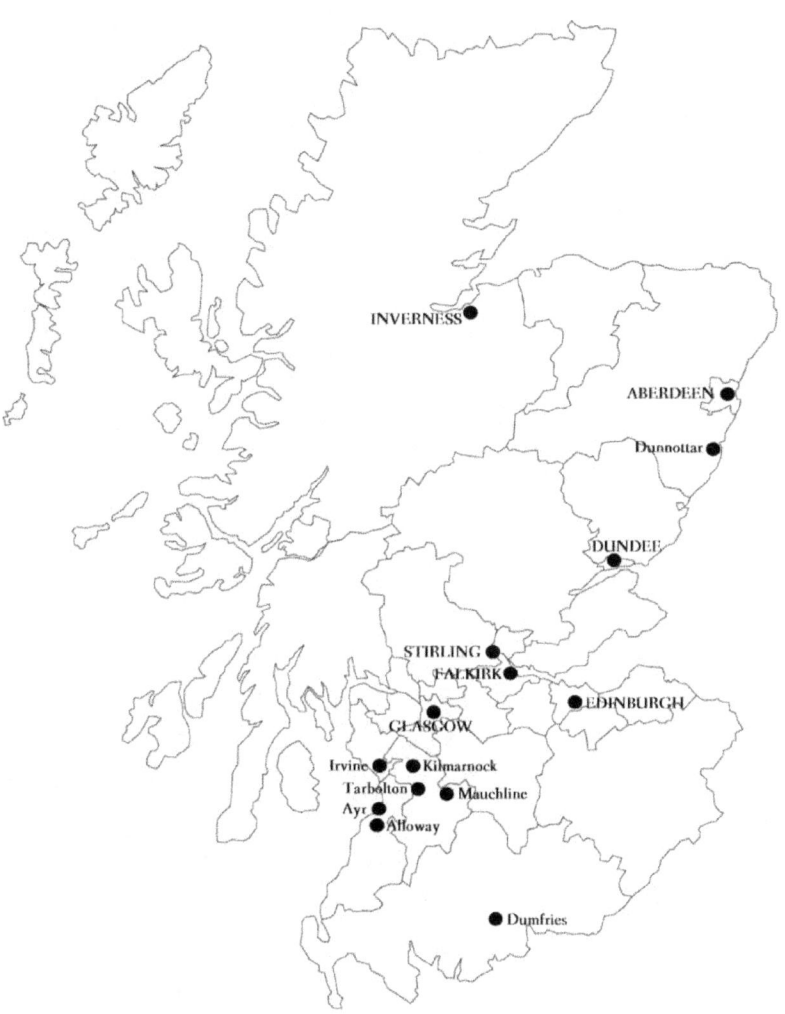

Cast photo of *The Spirit of Robbie Burns*, taken at a performance of the play staged at Auchmithie Church near Arbroath in February 2017.

Pictured from left to right: Garry Mitchell, Robert Murray, Rodger Brunton, Colette Dear, Jim Ramsay, Violet Thomson, James Hutcheson, Marina Kyle.

(Image Copyright © James Hutcheson, all rights reserved.)

Testimonials

"A refreshing change from the traditional Burns Supper format. An entertaining insight making great use of original letters to and from Burns. Songs and poems interwoven to give an account of the Bard's works. This is a well-balanced interpretation of Robert Burns' life story which audiences of all ages will learn from and enjoy."

Miss Helen Adam
Retired Carnoustie High School Teacher of English

"An interesting new take on the life of Robert Burns as seen through the eyes of the Bard himself. The three acts give one a clear insight into his personality and thinking during different stages of his short life."

Dr Hamish Leslie
Fintry, Stirlingshire

"Audiences remark on how much this theatrical presentation adds to their knowledge of Burns. Nicely balanced content of song, poetry and narrative. The characters in Burns' life come alive. All students of Robert Burns' works should see this."

Mr Jim Bates
Ilfracombe, North Devon

"This presentation of Burns' life is a must for all school children in Scotland and of Scottish descent to experience. The beauty about the format of this work is that it can be read or spoken, acted or not and with or without costume, props and staging. Ideal for any group, including schools."

Mr John Knox
Admirer of the Bard, and established speaker at Burns Suppers

"Over the years I have taken an active part in Burns Suppers, not only in Scotland but around the world, and I can honestly say my participation in this piece not only gave me an added knowledge of the Bard but took me on an emotional journey through his life."

Mr Rodger Brunton
Singer/Actor and Director/Producer of
Carnoustie Musical Society

"A well-researched stage presentation about Robbie Burns with a nice mix of his well-known material alongside lots of interesting facts which we rarely hear about. I have directed productions of this piece and received positive feedback from the actors and audiences alike."

Mr James Hutcheson
Director of musical shows

THE SPIRIT OF ROBBIE BURNS

Robert Murray

Preface

WELCOME to this, my first Burns book. I trust that you will find the play helpful as a means of presenting the life story of Robert Burns, and will enjoy many hours of rehearsing and performing it.

At the outset, I must emphasise that this play, or presentation, is written in a form such that it will be comfortable for experienced stage performers, amateur singers, and actors, as well as those who have never performed in public or in private.

I have provided guidance so that the show can be put on stage with each element of costume, stage props, and setting as described, or in fact with none of these aids. It can be adapted to suit any environment – professional stage, amateur theatre, or private home.

Over the years, I have attended Burns Suppers and Evenings with the traditional format of Toast to the Immortal Memory, Toast to the Lassies, and Reply on Behalf of the Lassies, with the appropriate songs and poems. And although the works of the Bard are presented, the life story of Rabbie is rarely told. This presentation is an attempt to tell his life story while including, at appropriate moments, his songs and poems.

I set out to write the life story of Robert Burns with the ultimate aim of writing a three-act play, complete with key figures in his life, but soon realised that his story would be so full as to require several plays.

My solution was to tell his story using narrators, with selected characters drawn from his life, and then to include songs and poems chronologically in the story. This, I think, gives a pleasing balance of acting, dialogue, narrating, singing, and reading.

The first performance was in Ilfracombe, North Devon in England, where I lived for several years and was involved with local drama and music groups.

The drama group traditionally had no stage production in January, and it was left for individual members to suggest an evening of some light entertainment. I had recently put together my play, and offered to fill the slot. I placed an item in the drama club's newsletter stating my intention to perform the life story of Burns, and was seeking a few colleagues to help narrate and sing. In the event, around 25 members answered the call, and so keen were they to become involved I had to invent small pieces of business on stage to include them. I incorporated a Burns Supper between Parts 1 and 2, and the show was performed on a small stage in a local hotel. A piano-playing member was briefed and parts allocated, and after two rehearsals we were ready to perform to the 70 ticket-holders. No costumes were used. To find that level of interest in an English seaside town was nothing short of a miracle, and the response was highly complimentary.

On returning to reside in my hometown of Carnoustie in Angus, Scotland, I casually discovered one evening that Dr Hamish Leslie, a friend, had been thinking for over 30 years of holding a Burns Supper in his home but had never got around to it. On telling him of my play, he quickly offered his house as a venue. Parts including narrators, singers, readers, and actors were allocated to our group of friends – numbering eleven – and each were sent a copy of the play with their parts marked. There was no rehearsal, no piano or special costume, and our Burns Supper took place after Part 1. As you will see, there are three parts to the story – Part 1 (Ayrshire) took place in Hamish's kitchen, Part 2 (Edinburgh) in his lounge, and Part 3 (Dumfries) in his living room. Hamish was thrilled, and we all felt we had told the story of Burns' life in an easy and entertaining fashion.

Since that memorable evening at Hamish's home, the play has been performed on several more occasions with a cast of experienced performers – once in a local hall with a stage in Carnoustie and four more in churches in the county of Angus, with further possible bookings into 2020.

This has proved to me that my story can be told with equal enjoyment by experienced stage performers and by those who have never in their lives stood up to speak, and this I believe is the success of my Burns life story format.

* * *

Dr Hamish Leslie and his wife Fiona, in whose home my Burns play was first performed in Scotland.
(Image reproduced by kind permission of Dr Hamish Leslie.)

You May Like To Know

In 1757, William Burns and his wife Agnes left Dunnottar, south of Stonehaven, to seek a new life in Ayrshire. They would have passed along the toll road a mere two miles from Carnoustie. Two years later, their son Robert was born.

Parish records in those days occasionally showed variations in family names, and the Burns surname was inadvertently altered to Burness or Burnes, or vice versa.

When I told Ian McDougall – my barber in Carnoustie for over 45 years – that I was writing this book, he informed me that his forbears, members of the Burns or Burness family, had moved from around the Dunnottar area to salmon fishing villages close to Carnoustie at Easthaven and Westhaven. He immediately quoted a verse of a poem handed down by his great-grandfather. Ian has no proof of his exact lineage and is reluctant to claim it may be a Burns piece, but what may be true is that the writing skills in his family are linked to the great man himself.

The verse Ian quoted to me while cutting my hair:

Nine o'clock the supper's spread
We hae a feed and aff tae bed
Five o'clock will soon be here
The cauld mornings mack you sweer.[1]

Running a successful newsagents shop, commencing at 4.30am each morning – and along with his barber's business for all his working years – Ian tells me he lived by that verse.

I know a successful young writer from Arbroath by the name of Louise Burness who is aware of her connection to Robert Burns, and so, once again, is there some evidence of a literary link to the area.

Louise has very kindly given me permission to include her own poetic words. As a descendent of Rabbie,

---

[1] Sweer means "unwilling".

she has caught the mood of a possible Burns view about a modern day 'micro meal':

> Behold, the ready meal for wan,
> The saddest sicht ye'll see,
> Prepackaged haggis, neeps and tatties,
> No fit for a Scots lass's tea.
> Fir naebody else likes haggis,
> Uncle Rabbie would turn in his grave,
> But then he'd raise his glass and say,
> But it's only fir the brave!

Very much in the Burns style; Rabbie's influence lives on! It's wonderful to know that those Burns family links are still in the world around us here in the county of Angus.

Robert Murray
Carnoustie, March 2019

For information about how to stage your own performance of The Spirit of Robbie Burns, *including sourcing permission from the author and details of necessary performance fees for theatrical groups, please visit Robert's website at* **www.robertmurrayauthor.co.uk**.

Statue of Robert Burns at Kilmarnock

(Image Credit: davy927tenpoleo at Pixabay)

Introductory Notes

THE main purpose of this book is to present to you a play, or presentation, about the life of Robert (or Rabbie) Burns.

The play is suitable to be performed by experienced performers, but I hope I am able to help those who have never taken part in any Burns evenings and to provide basic assistance to "put on your own show".

It may be performed in a hall, church, school, hotel, or in club premises, and it will take approximately one hour – depending on how much detail you decide to include.

However, for a full evening's entertainment a Burns Supper may be introduced between Parts 1 and 2.

Ideally, the play should be arranged to take place on or around the 25th of January, to coincide with "Burns Nicht". With that in mind, I have included details of how to arrange a full Burns evening. "Ready-made" speeches are included at the back of this book in the appendices section.

ORGANISING A BURNS SUPPER

Venue
You will need a hall or club room with a kitchen, or a hotel which has a function room – preferably with a small stage.

Stage
There is no need for special lighting or curtains. All that is required is a table and several chairs.

Function Room
Adequate tables and chairs, laid out in such a fashion that each guest can see the proceedings at the top table.

Guests
Traditionally this was all male, but today mixed company is preferred.

Top Table Plan
The top table (as viewed from the audience) should be arranged in the following fashion: **3 2 1 4 5**, with each role as follows:
1) Chairperson
2) Main speaker, 'Immortal Memory'
3) Toast, 'Reply from the Lassies'
4) Toast, 'To the Lassies'
5) Singer/poetry reader/minister to say Grace.

Dress
Robert Burns was a Lowlander, and is never seen in tartan. There are various forms of dress applicable to the entire company, and any one is equally acceptable:
a) Full evening dress
b) Lounge suit
c) Casual
d) A mix of the above
e) Tartan

(Of course, there could be a request that some small item of tartan in some form could be incorporated in a, b, c or d above.)

Although Burns never appears in tartan, it should be noted that he would have been aware of the fact that, following the Battle of Culloden in 1746, the British government passed the Dress Act of 1746 which banished clan chiefs and banned the wearing of tartan anywhere in Scotland. However, after that Act was repealed in 1782, tartan was again permitted. Since Rabbie had no good words to say about the Hanoverian King George III, he would have rejoiced at the change in the law allowing Scots to display their tartan heritage.

ORDER OF EVENTS AT A SUPPER

- Chairperson welcomes guests
- Piper pipes in the chef bearing the haggis, who presents it on the table in front of the person designated to "Address" the haggis (see Appendix I)
  (Note: A double whisky should be offered to the chef and piper who pipes the chef back to the kitchen)
- Church Minister, Club Official, or Volunteer says the "Selkirk Grace" (see Appendix II)
- The meal is served (see Appendix III)

- At the end of the meal, the Chairperson makes the Loyal Toast to the reigning Monarch (see Appendix IV)
- A Burns song or poem is performed
- Interval
- Chairperson introduces the "Immortal Memory" speaker (see Appendix V)
- Chairperson thanks the speaker and invites a speaker to "Toast the Lassies" (see Appendix VI)
- Chairperson invites a lady to "Reply from the Lassies" (see Appendix VII)
- A Burns song or poem will be performed
- Entire company upstanding to sing "Auld Lang Syne" (see Appendix VIII)
- The evening continues with or without any special plan

(Image Credit: Norman Pogson at Shutterstock)

The Spirit of Robert Burns

A Presentation of the Life of Robert Burns

Where Mr Burns returns 'in spirit'
as he recounts his life story
in narrative, song, poetry,
and theatrical dialogue

The Spirit of Robbie Burns
His Life Story in Three Parts

PART 1
AYRSHIRE, 1759 TO 1786
His young days at the plough and his early writing successes.

PART 2
EDINBURGH, 1786 TO 1788
Meeting the academic and literary giants of the day – and Clarinda!

PART 3
DUMFRIES, 1788 TO 1796
Farming again, and some of his best writing. Working hard to make ends meet.

Notes
The presentation will be enhanced if all the words can be spoken from memory. However, it may be read. Content of letters to and from Burns is authentic wording, taken from his original correspondence.

The content of each song or poem may be reduced to suit the required presentation and the time available.

BURNS' COSTUMES

In Act 1, distinctly dull and dark costume reflecting the poverty of his country life in Ayrshire. His shoes are well worn and look muddy.

In Act 2, the elegance and comfort of his high society life in Edinburgh should be reflected in his rich and colourful costume and polished black shoes with silver buckle.

In Act 3, his life as a farmer and a man of some means will be evident in his comfortable outfit of tweed trousers, high-length brown polished boots, and jacket.

Burns has returned "in spirit" to give us his feelings. As an option, therefore, his hands and face may be whitened to portray his ghost-like appearance.

ACT 1: "POVERTY IN AYRSHIRE"

The Stage
Interior of a dark, low ceilinged cottage, which has sparse furniture and no ornaments. Burns is seated at a small table with quill in hand, reading and editing his life story contained in a sheaf of papers tied together by a crimson ribbon.

Stage Props
Small, bare table and bench, papers, candle in saucer, quills in vase, books and papers scattered on table, beer mug.

Personal Props
Burns will have a small quill pen, ink jar and paper.

ACT 2: "HIGH SOCIETY IN EDINBURGH"

The Stage
The interior of a large room with signs of opulence.

Stage Props
A large brown leather chair and a large table covered by a colourful silk or similar cloth. A silver candelabra, oil lamp, crystal decanter, and port glass adorn the table. A large pot of quills along with books and papers sit on the table.

Personal Props
Burns uses a large quill pen and silver ink pot.

ACT 3: "FARMING LIFE IN DUMFRIES"

The Stage
Interior of a farmhouse living room.

Stage Props
A table now covered by a plain cloth and the chair is a comfortable carver. An oil lamp, plain pot of quills, beer tankard and books sit on the table

Personal Props
Burns uses a large quill pen and plain ink pot.

The Spirit of Robbie Burns was first performed by the Studio Theatre Group in Ilfracombe, North Devon, on the 20th of January 2007.

THE CAST
Narrators (one, two, or more)
Robert Burns
Alison Begbie
John Murdoch
The Rev. Dr Hugh Blair
Gilbert Burns
Clarinda
Jean Armour
William Burns

THE SONGS
(Accompanied by a pianist)
My Love is like a Red Red Rose
A Rosebud by my Early Walk
The Rigs o' Barley
Bonie Wee Thing
Afton Water
Ae Fond Kiss
A Man's a Man for a' That
The Banks o' Doon

THE POEMS
To a Mountain Daisy
The Fornicator
Death and Dr Hornbook

Willie
Will Ye go to The Indies, My Mary?
A Dream
Hen Pecked Country Squire
Rough Roads
Addressed to an Artist
Address to Edinburgh
Of A' the Airts the Wind Can Blaw
Verses to Clarinda
Tam O' Shanter
The Five Carlins
On Being asked Why God made Miss D so Little and Mrs A So Big
Marriage

The Spirit of Robbie Burns

Part I
Poverty in Ayrshire

Introduction: appropriate musical overture.

NARRATOR: Good evening everyone. We are going to take you back in time to the late 18th century in Scotland. With song, some well-known characters in his life – as well as verse – we will present some of the true facts and emotions of the life and works of Robert Burns. But surprise, surprise: I am delighted to tell you that we have with us Robbie Burns himself (or at least the 'spirit' of Robbie Burns)! So along with my friends on stage, we will give you an account of his life.

A great deal has been written about Burns, not all of it kind. He did not hide his weaknesses, nor evade the truth, and he certainly had a sense of humour.

He was born and bred within strict Calvinistic circumstances, and that gave him the courage and determination to promote a cause. Yes, that got him into a lot more trouble than the lassies! So here is Robbie, or Rabbie, or Robert Burns, speaking to us as he pens his life story...

BURNS: Good evening, my friends – my fellow literary enthusiasts! I am honoured that you are with me on this very special occasion. Aye; the anniversary of my birth.

You join me while I am reading and editing the rough notes I have made about my life. Of course, I am delighted to share these with you. Speaking from beyond this mortal coil, please forgive my rather ghostly appearance.

I also beg your forgiveness if I pause, momentarily, to reflect upon or amend a word or two as I proceed.

I am, Sirs/Madam, your obedient servant.

Now, did I hear someone say a moment or two ago that I, Robert Burns, had "weaknesses"?

Yes, I suppose I did give many indications of what my weaker points were – or, as my brother Gilbert used to say, "You have, my dear brother, one very strong characteristic!" and it sums up all the good and bad in me. That singular feature is "passion".

Yes. If I felt deeply about anything, I was usually very passionate. That applied to:

My ardent desire to learn and read.

My fervent passion about literature and writers.

My impassioned quest to learn about my fellow man.

My zealous wish to support the victim of circumstance, the poor, and those who suffer – especially through the rash acts of their fellow man.

And, yes – if I saw vanity, arrogance, boasting or hypocrisy I took great pleasure in lampooning, or exposing it.

My humour was satirical and gentle, but sometimes not so gentle – with scathing assaults on people and subjects which ranged from politics, religion, marriage, sex and even death.

My overwhelming conviction as an idealist was to be a voice in Scotland. To make an impression as a writer and poet, and a champion for fairness.

When I loved a lassie... yes, that was always hot-blooded and passionate. But my admissions at church were equally passionate!

I grew up in the countryside. I wrote about what I saw in my world and the characters and events around me. I looked closely and was astonished, at the beauty of nature.

POEM: "TO A MOUNTAIN DAISY"

Wee, modest crimson-tipped flow'r,
Thou's met me in an evil hour;
For I maun crush amang the stoure
Thy slender stem:
To spare thee now is past my pow'r,
Thou bonie gem.

Alas! It's no thy neibor sweet,
The bonie lark, companion meet,
Bending thee 'mang the dewy weet,

Wi' spreckl'd breast!
When upward-springing, blythe, to greet
The purpling east.

Cauld blew the bitter-biting north
Upon thy early, humble birth;
Yet cheerfully thou glinted forth
Amid the storm,
Scarce rear'd above the parent-earth
Thy tender form.

BURNS: My environment made me what I was. My life on this earth was short. I knew of only one King in my lifetime – George the Third. The monarchy was stable, despite the reign of a Hanoverian – and so-called madman. But there was hostility and uncertainty in politics, religion, and economics. The Union of the Crowns in 1603 and the Union of Parliaments in 1707 were all behind me. Times were troublesome and unpredictable, and it was the less fortunate in society who needed help.

Decisions by me were not by any means clever. Yes, I was ruled by my heart. I did seriously try to make all the right decisions about my farms, my family, and my publications. But when you are an enthusiastic visionary, a romantic, and overtaken by an inner unstoppable force, it's not easy to be down to earth and practical. I discovered I had a deep sentimental side to me. When I loved... yes, my friends, I dearly loved.

SONG: "MY LOVE IS LIKE A RED RED ROSE"

My love is like a red red rose
That's newly sprung in June;
My love is like the melodie
That's sweetly play'd in tune.
So fair art thou, my bonnie lass,
So deep in love am I;
And I will love thee still, my dear,
Till a' the seas gang dry.
Till a' the seas gang dry, my dear,
And the rocks melt wi' the sun:
And I will love thee still, my dear,
While the sands o' life shall run.
And fare thee weel, my only love
And fare thee weel, a while!
And I will come again, my love,
Tho' it were ten thousand mile.

NARRATOR: Robert Burns was born at Alloway, and lived in Ayrshire from 1759 until 1786. His father, William, had moved from Dunnotter, south of Aberdeen, and built his own "but and ben", or "auld clay biggin" – that is, a white-washed cottage with a thatched roof – at Alloway, Ayrshire. Robert, born on 25th January 1759 amidst a great storm, was the first of seven children and was blessed with a caring mother who ignited a furnace in young Robbie's mind with yarns, ancient poems, and ghostly stories. Robbie's father was determined to obtain the best education for his children, and engaged a young teacher, John Murdoch, to instruct children in the area with scholarly basics as well as the Classics, Latin, and French.

BURNS: In 1766, when I was not quite seven years old, my family moved to a farm at Mount Oliphant. By the age of fifteen, I was an experienced farm labourer on my father's land. This was a time of profound change for me. Father died, the estate factor was dealing most severely with financial arrears, and John Murdoch – my tutor – was sacked from his teaching job because he spoke out against a local church minister.

I found my first love. She was buxom Nelly Kirkpatrick. I was then just over fifteen years old. Later, when I was seventeen, my brother Gilbert and I were forced to move to another farm at Tarbolton. Sadly, poor farming ground and bad harvests were to constantly plague my family.

At this time my rhymes and songs were being noticed, and I began to hope that someday I may be able put an assemblage of my diverse works together.

SONG: "A ROSEBUD BY MY EARLY WALK"

A Rose-bud by my early walk,
Adown a corn-enclosed bawk,
Sae gently bent its thorny stalk,

All on a dewy morning.
Ere twice the shades o' dawn are fled,
In a' its crimson glory spread,
And drooping rich the dewy head,
It scents the early morning.

Within the bush her covert nest
A little linnet fondly prest;
The dew sat chilly on her breast,
Sae early in the morning.
She soon shall see her tender brood,
The pride, the pleasure o' the wood,
Amang the fresh green leaves bedew'd,
Awake the early morning.

So thou, dear bird, young Jeany fair,
On trembling string or vocal air,
Shall sweetly pay the tender care
That tents thy early morning.
So thou, sweet Rose-bud, young and gay,
Shalt beauteous blaze upon the day,
And bless the parent's evening ray
That watch'd thy early morning.

BURNS: I began to realise that earning a living off the land was not greatly successful. I had studied land surveying, and later, in Irvine, learned the flax trade to widen my skills in order to find other, more economic comfort. But these plans deserted me. I had fallen deeply in love with Nelly Kirkpatrick, and then even more fervently with a lass by the name of Peggy Thomson. A passionate affair with Alison Begbie followed. These situations came about, I think, because of my need to erase the memory of farming disasters and the failure to secure financial stability.

NARRATOR: On the 11th of November 1780, Burns started the Tarbolton Bachelor's Club. There were twelve members, and they debated many and varied local and national matters of interest and concern. A succession of work frustrations was not kind to Burns and he found himself in a state of melancholy, and so again he started to write. In 1785 he started a diary, and called it "My Common-Place Book". In it he recorded his observations, opinions, notions, and verse. It was at this time Burns seriously felt that he wanted to stamp his literary influence through poetry. His bias towards philosophy and serious deliberation was giving way to his burgeoning drive to write poetry.
The factor served sequestration on 17th May 1783 and seized the farm assets. Robbie and Gilbert were forced to move to Mossgiel – another farm. Their father had died on 13th February 1784, and so ended a doleful chapter at Tarbolton.

BURNS: A dreaded period indeed, but I found time to meet up with several lassies. Who? Well, as I said, there was Nelly, then Peggy, and of course the ever-amorous Annie.

SONG: "THE RIGS O' BARLEY"

It was upon a Lammas night,
When corn rigs are bonnie,
Beneath the moon's unclouded light,
I held awa to Annie:
The time flew by wi' tentless heed,
'Till, 'tween the late and early,
Wi' sma' persuasion she agreed
To see me thro' the barley.
Corn rigs, an' barley rigs,
An' corn rigs are bonnie:
I'll ne'er forget that happy night,
Amang the rigs wi' Annie.

The sky was blue, the wind was still,
The moon was shining clearly;
I set her down, wi' right good will,
Amang the rigs o' barley:
I ken't her heart was a' my ain;
I lov'd her most sincerely:
I kiss'd her owre and owre again,
Amang the rigs o' barley.

[*Chorus*]

BURNS: Ah yes! And then there was Alison Begbie. She was a domestic servant, and the daughter of a Galston farmer. It was she who inspired me to write *The Lass of Cessnock Banks*. We exchanged letters a few times, but – lo and behold – she jilted me. I was rejected. My attempts to repair the damaged relationship came to nothing. Rejection! This had never previously happened to me and I had no idea how to cope. Her letter of rebuff came to me:

ALISON: "Dearest Robert. I find my heart filled with joy at the very mention of your name. We have shared the most intimate of moments. Yet in truth, I must tell you – my dearest friend – I am unable to accept your offer to return to me. Thus, my friend, I feel I must endure life without you – but I wish you all kinds of happiness.

BURNS: I replied from Lochlie, in June 1781: "I ought in good manners to have acknowledged the receipt of your letter before this time, but my heart was so shocked at the contents of it, that I can scarcely yet collect my thoughts so as to write to you on the subject. I will not attempt to describe what I felt on receiving your letter. You wish me 'all kinds of happiness'. It would be weak and unmanly to say that without you I never can be happy; but sure I am, that sharing life with you, would have given it a relish, that, wanting you I can never taste".

NARRATOR: At Mossgiel, Robbie settled down to write – the years of 1785 and 1786, when aged 26 to 27, being his most productive. The closer proximity to the town of Mauchline meant that he could now socialise more, and his writings about the land were supplemented by his notes about people, gossip, and characters. Robert was stressed with the two elements in his life – his drive to write and bad luck – and experienced another period of disabling melancholy. Nevertheless, he found inspiration all around him, which provided a great store of imaginative material.

BURNS: Despite my troubles, I was enthused to write. I was helped by the generous time given to me by my highly regarded teacher John Murdoch, who kept an interest in my writing progress.
It was my discerning father and some far-sighted neighbours who had engaged John to teach me, Gilbert, and my friends. John was a brilliant guiding light for me, and I brushed up my English grammar. Sadly, he was accused (I believed falsely) of slander, and he went to London to teach French. He wrote to me just after the New Year in 1783...

MURDOCH: "My Dear Robert. It is the turn of year once again, and a time for one to reflect on one's achievements or otherwise. I heartily recall our many merry and learned gallops through the Classics, French language, and English grammar. You were one of my ablest pupils.

However, kind sir, I am pleased to enquire as to your literary prowess and your progress in the world of writing, and your joys in finding true expression of your thoughts, observations, and ideas. Pray, let me know your advances in this chosen honourable domain of dedication and skill. Lest this should comfort me in my aspirations for you, and my wish to see you soar in your literary pursuits."

BURNS: I replied to my former schoolmaster on the 15th of January 1783. "Dear Sir. I embrace it with pleasure to tell you that I have not forgotten, nor never will forget, the many obligations I lie under to your kindness and friendship.

I seem to be the one sent into the world, to see, and observe; and I very easily compound with the knave who tricks me of my money, if there be anything original about him which shows me human nature in a different light from anything I have seen before. In short, the joy of my heart is to 'study men, their manners and ways'. And for this darling subject, I cheerfully sacrifice every other consideration.

My favourite authors are of the sentimental kind, such as Shenstone – particularly his elegies; Thomson's *Man of Feeling*, a book I prize next to the Bible; *Man of the World*, Sterne, and McPherson's

Ossian – these are the glorious models after which I endeavour to form my conduct.

Dear Sir; your sincere friend, and obliged humble servant, Robert Burns.

NARRATOR: In 1784, a friend told Robbie that Elizabeth Paton's now obvious pregnancy was attracting attention and questions. She had been his mother's servant at Tarbolton. To quote the records, "she was a plain peasant worker, well-developed with a strong masculine understanding". Elizabeth was infatuated by Robert, and he responded in the way he knew best. On the 22nd of May 1785, a daughter was born. He, of course, was reprimanded by the Kirk Session and inevitably fined one guinea.

BURNS: I was always unwilling to take seriously the punishment meted out by the Kirk for fornication. I saw my sexuality as a higher virtue – yes, much loftier than religion. As I stated at the time. "I did not in the least feel ashamed to be on the cutty stool. I was more pre-occupied as to why I was there in the first place!" Nevertheless, I paid the fine – or as I referred to the penalty, as "the buttock hire".

NARRATOR: Robert's affair with Elizabeth and the birth of their child led to his first reprimand by the church. The couple were admonished by the minister while they stood side by side at the cutty stool and heard the charges. Burns failed to see any fornication at all, describing the situation as "The Blissful Joy of Lovers". The poem *The Fornicator* demonstrates Burns' defiance:

VERSE: "FORNICATOR"

Ye jovial boys who love the joys.
The blissful joys of Lovers;
Yet dare avow with dauntless brow,
When th' bony lass discovers;
Pray draw near and lend an ear,
And welcome in a Prater,
For I've lately been on quarantine,
A proven Fornicator.

Before the Congregation wide
I pass'd the muster fairly,
My handsome Betsey by my side,
We gat our ditty rarely;
But my downcast eye by chance did spy
What made my lips to water,
Those limbs so clean where I, between,
Commenc'd a Fornicator.

With rueful face and signs of grace
I pay'd the buttock-hire,
The night was dark and thro' the park
I could not but convoy her;

A parting kiss, what could I less,
My vows began to scatter,
My Betsey fell-lal de dal lal lal,
I am a Fornicator.
Your warlike Kings and Heroes bold,
Great Captains and Commanders;
Your mighty Caesars fam'd of old,
And Conquering Alexanders;
Fields they fought and laurels bought
And bulwarks strong did batter,
But still they grac'd our noble list
And ranked Fornicator!

BURNS: My life here at Mossgiel is more conducive than I could ever have imagined. Being closer to Mauchline is inspirational and I am writing more: about religious and political characters, and the social changes taking place around me. Ideas come to me while I am ploughing and at work on the farm. And now, I am a father! My daughter is a lovely little thing. My dear mother has agreed to bring up the lass within the family. I was inspired to write something:

SONG: "BONIE WEE THING"

Wishfully I look and languish
In that bonie face o' thine,
And my heart it stounds wi' anguish,
Lest my wee thing be na mine.

Chorus:
Bonie wee thing, cannie wee thing,
Lovely wee thing, wert thou mine,
I wad wear thee in my bosom,
Lest my jewel it should tine.

Wit, and Grace, and Love, and Beauty,
In ae constellation shine;
To adore thee is my duty,
Goddess o' this soul o' mine!

[*Repeat Chorus*]

NARRATOR: Robert and Gilbert attended a Masonic meeting in Tarbolton. It was Spring 1785, and the speaker that evening was the schoolmaster John Wilson who made a pretentious revelation of his medical knowledge. Mr Wilson had a grocery shop in the town, where he sold medications aided by a sign in the window stating: "Advice given for common disorders at the shop gratis". Robbie immortalised Mr Wilson's fanciful claims by composing a poem on his way home from the meeting. Burns' joke was that Wilson, whom he nicknamed Dr Hornbook, was assisting Death.

BURNS: I could not erase from my mind that there I was, toiling almost every day on the land with Gilbert, and here was "Death" gossiping with a ploughman on his way home after a night of joyful banter while Dr Hornbook and his risky medical experimenting is doing his job for him. My poem *Death and Dr Hornbook* is my humorous response to the subject of Death.

VERSE: "DEATH AND DOCTOR HORNBOOK"

Some books are lies frae end to end
And some great lies were never penn'd
Ev'n Ministers they hae been kenn'd
In holy rapture
A rousing whid, at times, to vend
And nail't wi' Scripture
But this that I am gaun to tell
Which lately on a night befel
Is just as true's the Deil's in hell
Or Dublin city
That e'er he nearer comes oursel
'S a muckle pity.

The Clachan yill had made me canty
I was na fou, but just had plenty
I stacher'd whyles, but yet took tent ay
To free the ditches
An' hillocks, stanes, an' bushes kenn'd ay
Frae ghaists an' witches
The rising Moon began to glowr
The distant Cumnock hills out-owre
To count her horns, wi' a' my pow'r
I set mysel

But whether she had three or four
I cou'd na tell.

BURNS: The Bachelor's Club and Mason's Lodge allow me the privilege of meeting some distinguished men – among them Dugald Stewart, Professor of Philosophy at Edinburgh, and Lord Selkirk. How and ever, the richest source of material for me are the taverns of Mauchline where I can reflect upon my vivid observations – especially of the numerous amusing characters. All this provides a treasure trove of interesting notes, and greatly advances my writing.

NARRATOR: In 1785, Robbie wrote another humorous poem. This time it was a satire on death and hypocrisy, and his target was the contemptible Willie Fisher. Willie, the hypocritical Calvinist church elder, died in 1809 when – in a snow storm – he fell into a ditch and died of exposure. He was reported as being drunk at the time, and Robbie – having passed away some thirteen years earlier – would have enjoyed the mockery in that. Willie was greatly satirised in *Holy Willie's Prayer*.

VERSE: "WILLIE"

Here Holy Willie's sair worn clay
Taks up its last abode;
His saul has ta'en some other way,

I fear, the left-hand road.

Stop! there he is, as sure's a gun,
Poor, silly body, see him;
Nae wonder he's as black's the grun,
Observe wha's standing wi' him.

Your brunstane devilship, I see,
Has got him there before ye;
But haud your nine-tail cat a wee,
Till ance you've heard my story.

Your pity I will not implore,
For pity ye have nane;
Justice, alas! has gi'en him o'er,
And mercy's day is gane.

But hear me, Sir, deil as ye are,
Look something to your credit;
A coof like him wad stain your name,
If it were kent ye did it.

BURNS: Wonders prevail! Now, I have fallen in love with a captivating lass by the name of Jean Armour. This time it is certainly the true love of my life!

Jean is pregnant, and her father, a master mason, is extremely angry. I have offered to marry her, but her father refuses to allow this and has ripped up my marriage contract.

> This brings me to the edge of hell yet again!
> I am viewed as a sinner, and seen as exercising careless judgement in the company I keep.
> Mr Armour opposes my future with Jean and sets his mind against me.

NARRATOR: Jean was sent to relatives in Paisley to have the baby. To diminish the pain, Burns offered to go to Jamaica and then return when the turmoil died. With his true love absent he felt the loss, but found consolation in the arms of Mary Campbell.

On the banks of the River Ayr in May, Robbie and Mary promised each other they would go to the West Indies together. They were betrothed to each other. She went home to the Western Isles to prepare, then travelled to Greenock to await his arrival. You can imagine his distress when he got there to find she had died of a fever!

BURNS: Here I am again. Nothing seems to go right for me? Farming? Searching for my truest love? Or just love? And am I going anywhere with my poetry? My melancholy has set in once more.

NARRATOR: Once again, Robert was suffering one of his many bouts of melancholy. He was heartened by the arrival of a letter from London, sent by his highly regarded teacher John Murdoch.

BURNS: In these most depressing times, when my heart is heavy and spirits low I rejoice at the receipt of a letter from my most esteemed tutor:
"My Dear Sir. London, 28th October 1787.
I flatter myself, however, with the pleasing thought that you and I shall meet sometime or other in Scotland or England. If ever you come hither, you will have the satisfaction of seeing your poems relished by the Caledonians in London full as much as they can be by those of Edinburgh. We frequently repeat some of your verses in our Caledonian Society; and you may believe that I am not a little vain that I have had some share in cultivating such a genius.
Present my respectful compliments to Mrs Burns, to my dear friend Gilbert and all the rest of her amiable children. May the father of the Universe bless you all.
I am, my dear friend, yours sincerely, John Murdoch."

BURNS: What more could a man wish for than to receive such acclaim from one such learned gentleman as John Murdoch? I am indeed blessed with his presence in my life.

VERSE: "WILL YE GO TO THE INDIES, MY MARY?"

Will ye go to the Indies, my Mary,
And leave auld Scotia's shore?
Will ye go to the Indies, my Mary,
Across th' Atlantic roar?

O sweet grows the lime and the orange,
And the apple on the pine;
But a' the charms o' the Indies
Can never equal thine.

I hae sworn by the Heavens to my Mary,
I hae sworn by the Heavens to be true;
And sae may the Heavens forget me,
When I forget my vow!

O plight me your faith, my Mary,
And plight me your lily-white hand;
O plight me your faith, my Mary,
Before I leave Scotia's strand.

We hae plighted our troth, my Mary,
In mutual affection to join;
And curst be the cause that shall part us!
The hour and the moment o' time!

NARRATOR: Robbie returned to Mauchline a dejected man and, sitting in 'sinner's sackcloth', was severely reprimanded from the pulpit on three consecutive Sundays. Mr Armour, a severe man with a reputation to keep intact, had broadcast his failings!

Robbie was determined to sail to the West Indies, where he had secured a post as book-keeper in Jamaica at £30 per annum. He remained at home while his collection of poems was printed, and until he had a ship. In September Jean gave birth to twins.

His collection of poems was duly printed in Kilmarnock, and became known as the Kilmarnock Edition. This was the highest and brightest moment he had longed for.

One other way in which Robbie penned his humour was to attack class and royalty. On King George's birthday, it was the custom for some poets to dedicate a flattering birthday ode. On the 4th of June 1786, George the Third was 48 years old, and Robbie insisted on including a less sincere ode in the Kilmarnock Edition. When told it may damage his early and promising future, he replied: "I set as little by Kings, Lords, clergy as all these respectable people do by my bardship".

In the poem, Robert dreamed he had spoken to the King and criticised his policies over legislation and taxation. He also criticised the Royal Family, and especially the Duke of York for his indiscretions. "May you all experience the real hunger that your people endure." But it is all said with sarcasm and humour. Robert had little respect for the Hanoverians.

VERSE: "A DREAM"

Guid-Mornin' to our Majesty!
May Heaven augment your blisses
On ev'ry new birth-day ye see,
A humble poet wishes.
My bardship here, at your Levee
On sic a day as this is,
Is sure an uncouth sight to see,
Amang thae birth-day dresses
Sae fine this day.

I see ye're complimented thrang,
By mony a lord an' lady;
"God save the King"'s a cuckoo sang
That's unco easy said aye:
The poets, too, a venal gang,
Wi' rhymes weel-turn'd an' ready,
Wad gar you trow ye ne'er do wrang,
But aye unerring steady,
On sic a day.

For me! before a monarch's face
Ev'n there I winna flatter;
For neither pension, post, nor place,
Am I your humble debtor:
So, nae reflection on your Grace,
Your Kingship to bespatter;
There's mony waur been o' the race,
And aiblins ane been better

Than you this day.

'Tis very true, my sovereign King,
My skill may weel be doubted;
But facts are chiels that winna ding
An' downa be disputed:
Your royal nest, beneath your wing,
Is e'en right reft and clouted,
And now the third part o' the string,
An' less, will gang aboot it
Than did ae day.

Far be't frae me that I aspire
To blame your legislation,
Or say, ye wisdom want, or fire,
To rule this mighty nation:
But faith! I muckle doubt, my sire,
Ye've trusted ministration
To chaps wha in barn or byre
Wad better fill'd their station
Than courts yon day.

And now ye've gien auld Britain peace,
Her broken shins to plaister,
Your sair taxation does her fleece,
Till she has scarce a tester:
For me, thank God, my life's a lease,
Nae bargain wearin' faster,
Or, faith! I fear, that, wi' the geese,
I shortly boost to pasture

I' the craft some day.

An' Will's a true guid fallow's get,
(A name not envy spairges),
That he intends to pay your debt,
An' lessen a'your charges;
But, God-sake! Let nae saving fit
Abridge your bonie barges
An' boats this day.
I'm no mistrusting Willie Pitt,
When taxes he enlarges.

BURNS: I was aware that, by my words, I had been branded a traitor and my good name sullied. However, I felt strongly that the lavishly rich life of the select few in the country was at odds with the poverty and hardship of the vast majority. My so-called attacks were not only confined to the rich and famous, but to some other, less obvious subjects which were ripe for a piece of my tongue – or, should I say, by "the barb of my pen".

NARRATOR: Now, we see another example of Robbie bringing humour to Death. He wrote an epitaph which was inspired by the death of William Campbell of Mauchline, who died in 1786. In this short verse, Robert pities Campbell for his demanding wife.

VERSE: "HEN PECKED COUNTRY SQUIRE"

As father Adam first was fool'd,
(A case that's still too common,)
Here lies man a woman ruled,
The devil ruled the woman.

NARRATOR: Robbie's waggish humour is also contained in an epigram entitled *Rough Roads*, which is a scoff at both religion and work. This may relate to the road between Kilmarnock and Stewarton.

VERSE: "ROUGH ROADS"

I'm now arrived-thanks to the gods! –
Thro' pathways rough and muddy,
A certain sign that makin' roads
Is no this people's study:
Altho' I'm not wi' Scripture cram'd,
I'm sure the Bible says
That heedless sinners shall be damn'd,
Unless they mend their ways.

BURNS: I felt I had established a sound foundation as a writer, and confidence came my way. I began to write about the many aspects of life in Ayrshire, and I was greatly pleased with my stock of writing material.

I had experienced a fertile work period, and yet at times suffered melancholy periods. My Common-Place Book was filled. I needed the money badly, but most of all I had that burning ambition – as I had often said – "to see my work in guid black print".

The Kilmarnock Edition of July 1786 was entitled *Scotch Poems by Robert Burns*. One volume, octavo stitched; three shillings, 240 pages. There were 612 copies printed, and only 13 copies left unsold at the end of August. A profit of £20!

Questionable words of satire and contention were excluded, the contents dwelling mainly on life on the land and in the villages – and of course my loves, romances and emotions.

NARRATOR: The response from every city, town and village in the land was loud and clear: "Give us more!" There was such a dearth of popular Scottish reading material that, from every level of society, the Edition was digested across the country. Robbie Burns' genius had resonated with rural Scotland, and his followers could relate to his brilliance in describing what they experienced and felt. Invitations came in sack-loads to do a second edition through an Edinburgh publisher, and the literati of Edinburgh were most favourably impressed.

BURNS: At last my strenuous efforts are bearing fruit! My dark preoccupations and sorrow are gone! My poetry is hailed a success! How I wish my father could have witnessed this!

I must purchase some gentlemanly attire, for I am on my way to the Capital. I have decided it is time for me to enjoy my place "at the table of life".

I have borrowed a pony, and leave for Edinburgh on the 27th of November.

Closing piano music.

INTERVAL

[*If no interval is planned, some appropriate music may be considered while props are changed.*]

The Spirit of Robbie Burns

Part II
High Society in Edinburgh

Opening piano music.

BURNS: Ah! This high social scene of Edinburgh! What will it offer me? Alluring attractions, inveiglements and dangers! Could this pulsating environment damage my writing... or, more likely, damage me?

I sense my readers may expect me to celebrate and exalt the Scottish spirit through story, song, and satire. My concern is that whatever I have done has been by my close contact with nature and local characters. Edinburgh is a wonderful spur, scholarly and hospitably, but perhaps a dangerous influence for my writing. Will I lose my touch? That feel for the rural countryside, and the people who are the salt of the earth?

Whatever; here I am on a surge of delight and a wave of passion that I could only ever have dreamed of. I am a spectacle in the great city! But, but, and yes, BUT! "I am only too well aware of being a meteor – aye, quick to burst into dazzling brilliance, but equally quick to fade away!" Yes. I must add that cautionary note!

NARRATOR: Robbie's everlasting leaning to his humorous side was still very much to the fore. While visiting an artist in Edinburgh in the late part of 1786, he was moved to write an epigram on the back of a small sketch. The painter was working on a picture of Jacob's Dream at the time, and this was Robbie's poke at religion in his own fashion.

VERSE: "ADDRESSED TO AN ARTIST"

Dear Sir, I'll gie ye some advice,
You'll tak it no uncivil:
You shouldna paint at angels mair,
But try and paint the devil.

To paint an angel's kittle wark,
Wi' Nick, there's little danger:
You'll easy draw a lang-kent face,
But no sae weel a stranger.

NARRATOR: On the 14th of January 1787, The Grand Master Mason of Scotland proposed a toast in honour of Robert Burns, to "Caledonia and Caledonia's Bard, Brother Burns". Burns found himself hosted as a special guest in the grandest of homes in the city.

Alcohol was everywhere; the whole scene was one of merriment and socialising. During daytime, the inns were packed. Flats were too small in which to carry on business, so doctors, lawyers, and merchants saw their clients and customers in a tavern. The whole place brimmed with frenzied business dealings.

The house of influential publisher, Mr William Creech, was both his lending library and publishing offices. Each day men of highest literary prowess met there to discuss political and economic news.

Burns' second edition is to be published by Creech. He corrected proofs from December to April.

POEM: "ADDRESS TO EDINBURGH"

Edina! Scotia's darling seat!
All hail thy palaces and tow'rs,
Where once beneath a Monarch's feet,
Sat Legislation's sov'reign pow'rs!
From marking wildly-scatt'red flow'rs,
As on the banks of Ayr I stray'd,
And singing, lone, the ling'ring hours,
I shelter in thy honour'd shade.

Here Wealth still swells the golden tide,
As busy Trade his labours plies;
There Architecture's noble pride
Bids elegance and splendour rise:
Here Justice, from her native skies,
High wields her balance and her rod;
There Learning, with his eagle eyes,
Seeks Science in her coy abode.

NARRATOR: Burns had never enjoyed such rich fellowship. He found, within half a mile of his lodgings, he could meet with numerous renowned men of the literary world. He enjoyed the mingling and the debate which followed with his fellow writers and authors. He enjoyed an abundance of questions and answers.

He had arrived on a borrowed pony and knew only a few people, and now here he was chatting freely with numerous new high-ranking friends and acquaintances in almost every educational discipline in Scotland's greatest city.

At this time in history Edinburgh displayed an inclusive, healthy attitude where all shades of political and social opinion could meet in harmony. This "brotherhood of man" was very much in keeping with Burns' own democratic feelings, and he witnessed the dynamic power of it at work in the arts. Despite the distractions around him, Burns found the inclination to commence a second "Common-Place Book".

He was overjoyed by the acknowledgement of his literary efforts by none other than the highly respected man of letters, The Reverend Dr Hugh Blair. A very distinguished man, he had graduated MA at Edinburgh and was licensed to preach at St Giles High Kirk. He was Professor of Rhetoric at Edinburgh University, and played a key part in the Age of Enlightenment. Despite the age difference and the gap in social position, Dr Blair was one of Burns' warmest admirers.

Hugh Blair wrote to him as follows:

BLAIR: "Dear Sir. Argyll Square, Edinburgh. 4th May, 1787. The success you have met with I do not think was beyond your merits; and if I have had any small hand in contributing to it, it gives me great pleasure. I know of no way in which literary persons, who are advanced in years, can do more service in the world than in forwarding the efforts of rising genius or bringing forth unknown merit from obscurity.

Dear Sir, yours sincerely, Hugh Blair."

NARRATOR: Such admiration was proof for Robert that his works were now recognised not only by people in the countryside, but also by the highest intellects in the land.

BURNS: I am completely enthralled to be here in the pulsating capital, but my thoughts return often to the landscape I know so well.

SONG: "AFTON WATER"

Flow gently, sweet Afton, amang thy green braes
Flow gently, I'll sing thee a song in thy praise
My Mary's asleep by thy murmuring stream
Flow gently, sweet Afton, disturb not her dream

Thou stock dove whose echo resounds through the glen
Ye wild whistling blackbirds in yon thorny den
Thou green-crested lapwing, thy screaming forbear
I charge you, disturb not my slumbering fair
How pleasant thy banks and green valleys below
Where wild in the woodlands the primroses blow
There oft, as mild evening weeps over the lea
Thy sweet-scented birks shade my Mary and me
Thy crystal stream, Afton, how lovely it glides
And winds by the cot where my Mary resides
How wanton thy waters her snowy feet lave
As, gathering sweet flowerets, she stems thy clear wave
Flow gently, sweet Afton, amang thy green braes
Flow gently, sweet river, the theme of my lays
My Mary's asleep by thy murmuring stream
Flow gently, sweet Afton, disturb not her dream.

NARRATOR: It was in Edinburgh at this time when the young Sir Walter Scott met Robert Burns at only sixteen years of age. Scott was to record later his impressions of that famous meeting with Robert:

"I found him to be a strong robust figure with a dignified plainness. He was a man of strong expression – his eyes glowed when he spoke with feeling or interest. I never saw such an eye in a human head," wrote Scott. "In conversation he was confident without presumption, and amongst the top men of his time he expressed himself with firmness and modesty."

The Edinburgh Edition was going well, with three thousand copies sold and further editions to follow! Burns then worked with James Johnson to put together a collection of Scottish songs.

Robert had seen an extraordinary period in Edinburgh, and now had to plan what followed. Go back to his Mauchline roots, or take up an offer of a farm near Dumfries?

But he now had the means to take his time to see Scotland, and he planned a series of tours. These took up almost all of 1787. He visited the Borders, the South West, Argyll and Loch Lomond, and then undertook his grand tour of Perthshire and the Highlands before heading back to Edinburgh along the East Coast.

BURNS: I must remind myself that my roots are in the Ayrshire countryside. I have sampled the delightfully demanding social whirl of Edinburgh, and my new-found wealth allows me for the first time to see the beauty of Scotland. And yet, I constantly feel drawn to my native heath.

NARRATOR: An exchange of correspondence between Burns and his brother Gilbert gives an insight to his grand tour. Gilbert was a dependable and faithful brother to Burns, as well as being a partner in their farming activities at Mossgiel. He was two years younger than Burns, and a hardworking man who had been left to manage the farm and support the family. It is worth noting John Murdoch always thought that Burns was least likely to excel in poetry and prose, as he was of a more serious demeanour. Gilbert, on the other hand, appeared to John as having a more lively imagination than Burns.

GILBERT: "My Dear Brother Robert. 14th August, 1787.
I pen this letter of enquiry in the full hope that you may receive same on your return to the Capital. We keep ourselves fully occupied by preparing for the harvest, though I doubt even with the Lord's help we will see any small part of a good one this year. We are in need of news pertaining to your travels, and in which respect how your good health holds.
So that I may let our dearest families know of your unusual and demanding travel experiences, please be kind enough to furnish me with details.
I am Sir, your Admiring brother, Gilbert."

BURNS: "My Dear Brother. Edinburgh, 17th September, 1787.
Having started out on the 25th of August, I arrived here safe yesterday evening after a tour of twenty-two days, and travelling near six hundred miles. Windings included. My farthest stretch was about ten miles beyond Inverness. I went through the heart of the Highlands by Crieff, Taymouth (the

famous seat of Lord Breadalbane), down the Tay to Dunkeld (seat of the Duke of Athole), thence to Blair of Athole – another of the Duke's seats. Thence through wild country and savage glens to Speyside to Grant castle, where I spent half a day with Sir James Grant and his family. Then on to Fort George, calling in at Cawdor – the ancient seat of Macbeth – where I saw an identical bed in which Duncan was slain. Then on to Inverness.

I returned by the coast route: Nairn, Forres, Aberdeen, Stonehive, and thence to Montrose, where James Burness met me by appointment.

You shall hear further from me before I leave Edinburgh.

My duty and many compliments from the North to my Mother, and my brotherly compliments to the rest.

Farewell, Your loving Brother Robert."

NARRATOR: Burns was accompanied on his Highland tour by William Nicol, who was the arrogant classics master at the High School of Edinburgh where he had a reputation for the wickedly frequent and cruel use of the cane. While on their travels, Robert had to bear Nicol's obnoxious attitude and behaviour with some calm – although it is on record that he did embarrass Robert on many high ranking occasions.

While on one of his tours, he went back to Mauchline. He had left the place penniless and with a doubtful reputation and returned a rich and famous man – acclaimed wherever he travelled! He renewed contact with Jean, the mother of his twins, but the family were still very uncertain about him.

Yet again he began to experience a melancholy period. What was the future? Had Edinburgh driven a wedge between him and his roots? Would this remove his stimulation to write as before?

Burns returned to Edinburgh for a second winter, but this time his acclamation was replaced by prolonged anxiety caused by the difficult commercial behaviour of his publisher, Mr Creech, which damaged their working relationship. Robert had been introduced to his publisher by the Earl of Glencairn, who was a very good friend of Creech – a man who, being Lord Provost, was held in very high regard by the establishment in Edinburgh. Robbie sold him his copyright for 100 guineas, but the skinflint Creech delayed the publication and the sums due to be paid to Burns. However, Burns later turned the tables by writing about Creech's long-standing money grabbing reputation.

BURNS: "Sir. 24th January, 1788.

When a business, which could at any time be done in a few hours, has kept me four months without even a shadow of anything else to do but wait on it, 'tis no very favourable symptom that it will be soon done, when I am a hundred miles absent. At any rate, I have no mind to make the experiment, but am determined to have it done before I leave Edinburgh. But why should I go into the country till I clear with you? I don't know what to do or what I have in my power to do. You have declared yourself to the public at large my friend, my patron; at all times I gratefully own it. I beg you will continue to be so and rather make a little exertion amid your hurried time than trifle with a poor man in his very existence; I shall expect to hear from you tomorrow, or next day, and have the honour to be, Sir, your very humble servant."

NARRATOR: Along with these problems with Creech, Robbie was preoccupied by worries about Jean and their life ahead. He genuinely loved Jean, but couldn't see a way of planning their future together.

The following verse was about Jean:

VERSE: "OF A' THE AIRTS THE WIND CAN BLAW"

Of a' the airts the wind can blaw,
I dearly like the west,
For there the bonie lassie lives,
The lassie I lo'e best:

There's wild-woods grow, and rivers row,
And mony a hill between:

But day and night my fancys' flight
Is ever wi' my Jean.

I see her in the dewy flowers,
I see her sweet and fair:
I hear her in the tunefu' birds,
I hear her charm the air:
There's not a bonie flower that springs,
By fountain, shaw, or green;
There's not a bonie bird that sings,
But minds me o' my Jean.

BURNS: Yes, Jean – my bonnie Jean. That's where I wanted to be, but I had met in Edinburgh a lady of some high standing and intellect. We found a common interest in literature. We were soul mates; we shared our humour and enjoyed discussion on almost all subjects. Her name was Mrs Agnes McLehose. Her husband – a dishonoured Glasgow solicitor – had, after a wild romance, married her but was now in the West Indies and had long since neglected his duties as a husband. Agnes and I met regularly, and corresponded almost daily – yes, aye, and on occasions hourly. We assumed identities; this was to protect Agnes' financial income, which she received from her cousin Lord Craig. Her identity could have been exposed at any time, and this seemed to add to our intrigue. Thus she became "Clarinda" and I, "Sylvander".

NARRATOR: Robbie had met with some bonnie lasses. Some with only a mild interest in poetry and literature, but usually not. The great attraction for Robert was their physical attributes rather than their intellectual qualities. Mrs McLehose was one lady with whom he shared an interest in writing, and this – combined with her physical beauty – captured his heart in a unique way. She was a high society lady. She had married the Glasgow solicitor James McLehose, who was physically abusive towards her. She had fled the marital home and he had emigrated to Jamaica to seek a new life.
She and Robbie each had an immediate infatuation with each other. However, the relationship was entirely platonic. Robbie's attempts to seek her as a close supportive partner failed.

BURNS: Our relationship was one of intense love and mutual admiration and yet, because of her circumstances, all we were ever able to do was to declare our feelings with no physical contact and thus no future together. She wrote to me at eleven o'clock on the morning of Tuesday the 15th of January 1788.

CLARINDA: "My Sylvander. I am some whiles caught in the most dreadful feeling of helplessness. I have my children to think of, and yet I have to question my love for their absent papa and my husband who is somewhere on the other side of the world.

I have to question my integrity and yes, my deeds. Yet whilst I carry these burdens it is with you that I desire by choice to spend my time in this Capital. Our shared interests, our common views and purpose... and yet, I cannot in all honesty give my whole being to you. My passion is certainly in my head and heart, but alas not in my body. My state of confusion brings me to weep even as I write. I wish not to offend you."

BURNS: "My darling Clarinda. Tuesday evening, 15th January, 1788.

You talk of weeping, Clarinda; some involuntary drops wet your lines as I read them. Offend me, my dearest Angel! You cannot offend me.

That you have faults, Clarinda, I never doubted; but I knew not where they existed, and Saturday night made me in the dark than ever. O' Clarinda, why would you wound my soul by hinting that last night must have lessened my opinion of you! True, I was 'behind the scenes with you', but what did I see? A bosom glowing with honour and benevolence; a mind ennobled by genius, informed and refined by education and reflection; a heart formed for all the glorious meltings of friendship, love and pity.

Do allow me to wait on you for Saturday next. Oh, my Angel! When we shall meet again? Sylvander."

VERSE: "VERSES TO CLARINDA"
(sent with a pair of crystal glasses)

Fair Empress of the Poet's soul,
And Queen of Poetesses;
Clarinda, take this little boon,
This humble pair of glasses:

And fill them up with generous juice,
As generous as your mind;
And pledge them to the generous toast,
"The whole of human kind!"

"To those who love us!" second fill;
But not to those whom we love;
Lest we love those who love not us –
A third – "To thee and me, Love!"

BURNS: Alas, there came a moment when we each realised we were trapped in our respective situations. She set off to reconcile with her husband and salvage the marriage, and I – well, I knew my heart was with Jean... and Clarinda was aware of that!

With huge emotion we said our farewells on the 6th of December 1791, which were final, and we never again met. We had cross-examined the depths of our souls, exchanged heart-felt feelings and pondered on a future together, but we both had to accept the inevitable.

SONG: "AE FOND KISS"

Ae fond kiss, and then we sever;
Ae fareweel, alas, for ever!
Deep in heart-wrung tears I'll pledge thee,
Warring sighs and groans I'll wage thee!
Who shall say that Fortune grieves him
While the star of hope she leaves him?
Me, nae cheerfu' twinkle lights me,
Dark despair around benights me.
I'll ne'er blame my partial fancy;
Naething could resist my Nancy;
But to see her was to love her,
Love but her, and love for ever.
Had we never loved sae kindly,
Had we never loved sae blindly,
Never met – or never parted,
We had ne'er been broken-hearted.
Fare thee weel, thou first and fairest!
Fare thee weel, thou best and dearest!
Thine be ilka joy and treasure,
Peace, enjoyment, love, and pleasure!
Ae fond kiss, and then we sever!
Ae fareweel, alas, for ever!
Deep in heart-wrung tears I'll pledge thee,
Warring sighs and groans I'll wage thee!

NARRATOR: We can only imagine the despair of Robert losing Clarinda. The experience, however, had clarified his thoughts, and he set off to

Mauchline and his true love Jean. He found a position as a trainee Excise Officer, and signed a lease for Ellisland Farm near Dumfries. His Edinburgh experiences had been boisterous and enlightening, and now he was, as they say, "back to auld cla'es and porridge" – the real world!

BURNS: My return to Jean reminded me of her virtues: her generosity, kindness and reliable influence in my life. We lived together at Mauchline for a while, and we married on the 5th of August 1788. Looking back, I was in an agreeable relationship with Elizabeth Paton when I was captivated by Jean during Race Week. She was one of the "Mauchline Belles", and it wasn't long before we were intimate and she became pregnant. I took on my responsibility and offered to marry Jean, but her father destroyed our contract. Jean went to Paisley to have the baby. I had an affair with Mary Campbell, and I had to set my mind on emigrating to Jamaica. I had many a dalliance after Mary; there was May Cameron, Jenny Clow, and Clarinda. Then, joy of joys, Jean presented me with twins. Despite this, her father began to see my qualities as a writer, and his attitude towards me improved.

NARRATOR: An exchange of letters between Jean and the Bard gives a touching insight to their gentle and genuine closeness.

JEAN: "My Dearest Husband. Mauchline, 9th October, 1788.

I am fearful for your good health, my dear Robert. Please take great care, as with the approach of winter you will need to be established in a safe and warm place. I must declare that I do not enjoy these long separations, and I will wish to walk the road to meet you on Sunday on your way home.

Pray, what is the news of the apples? I would be most grateful to hear news of your plans for Nithsdale, for as the cold and dark days close in we may find ourselves disadvantaged.

I am, ever, your faithful loving wife and servant, Jean."

BURNS: "My Dearest Love. Ellisland, Tuesday 14th October, 1788.

You need not come on Sunday to meet me on the road, for I am engaged that day to dine with Mr Logan at Laycht, so it will be in the evening before I arrive at Mauchline.

You must be ready for Nithsdale as fast as possible, for I have an offer of a house in the very neighbourhood with some furniture in it, all of which I shall have the use of for nothing till my own house be got ready.

We will want a maid servant of consequence; if you can hear of anyone to hire, ask after them.

The apples are all sold and gone. I am extremely happy at the idea of your coming to Nithsdale, as it will save us from these cruel separations.
I am, ever, my dearest madam, your faithful husband and humble servant,
Robert Burns."

Appropriate music while props are changed.

The Spirit of Robbie Burns

Part III
Farming Life in Dumfries

NARRATOR: Situated on the west bank of the River Nith and six miles from Dumfries, Ellisland was an unsurpassable place for a poet. Sadly, what Burns was not aware of was that he had signed for the poorest of two farms, for Ellisland would never provide a living income.

A sad repeat of his earlier farming disasters. But the peace and tranquillity of the area gave him the opportunity to pick up the pen again. It was here that he wrote one of his most loved works, *Tam O' Shanter*.

VERSE: "TAM O' SHANTER"

When chapman billies leave the street,
And drouthy neibors, neibors, meet;
As market days are wearing late,
And folk begin to tak the gate,
While we sit bousing at the nappy,
An' getting fou and unco happy,
We think na on the lang Scots miles,
The mosses, waters, slaps and stiles,
That lie between us and our hame,

Where sits our sulky, sullen dame,
Gathering her brows like gathering storm,
Nursing her wrath to keep it warm.

NARRATOR: Free of financial worries and romantic dalliances, Robbie could be at long last a happy family man. His two sons arrived – oh yes, and an illegitimate daughter born in Leith, whose mother was the niece of the landlady of the Globe Inn at Dumfries. Jean in her kindly way agreed to take the child into the family.

After three and a half years, Robert and the family moved into Dumfries town. He gave up farming and went full-time into the Excise service. His first appointment in August 1789 gave him an annual salary of fifty pounds. He was required to visit ten parishes, by fourteen journeys, covering thirty to forty miles on horseback each day. He received no expenses, and was required to provide his own horse. All his paperwork had to be done in the evenings. Many, in all levels of society in the land, questioned why their National Bard should be reduced to this state.

In October 1789, Sir James Johnston and a Captain Miller were contesting the Parliamentary election in Dumfries, and Robbie – still actively writing, despite the rigours of his job – penned this account of the campaign promoted by the Carlin family.

VERSE: "THE FIVE CARLINS"

There was five Carlins in the South,
They fell upon a scheme,
To send a lad to London town,
To bring them tidings hame.

Not only bring them tidings hame,
But do their errands there,
And aiblins gowd and honor baith
Might be that laddie's share.

There was Maggy by the banks o' Nith,
A dame wi' pride enough;
And Marjory o' the mony Lochs,
A Carlin auld and teugh :

And blinkin Bess of Annandale
That dwelt on Solway-side;
And Brandy Jean, that took her gill,
In Galloway sae wide.

And black Joan frae Crichton-peel,
O' gipsey kith and kin:
Five wighter Carlins were na found
The South Coontrie within.

To send a lad to London town,
They met upon a day;
Ad mony a knight and mony a laird

That errand fain wad gae.

NARRATOR: Despite the tiring work and oft-times wretched weather in which he had to work, Burns found time to set up the Monkland reading and lending library group and to deal with the numerous manuscripts sent to him by aspiring writers. He now had time to reflect on the favourable impact of his writings and observe how his works had inspired others. He involved himself with the Dumfries Theatre, and made time to write. The French Revolution became a threat, and troops were spread about the country. A Corps of Volunteers was raised, and Burns enlisted as a Private. In addition to all of that, he also found time to complete his work and publish the *Scots Musical Museum*.

For the first time in his life, Robert Burns enjoyed the completeness of all he held dear: his family, his house, the theatre, The Globe Tavern, and the reading rooms. He enjoyed the many town events. At the end of a working day, he would sit in the back room of the Globe, where people from many miles away came to hear him. The backcloth to his time there was the French Revolution, and a popular demand in Scotland for wider democracy. The old order controlled by the landed class was challenged. Burns, by nature, was a democrat. Trade Unions were forbidden. The Government forbade any moves to widen democracy, and this was completely at odds with Burns' sense of liberty and equality.

SONG: "A MAN'S A MAN FOR A' THAT"

Is there for honest Poverty
That hings his head, an' a' that;
The coward slave-we pass him by,
We dare be poor for a' that!
For a' that, an' a' that.
Our toils obscure an' a' that,
The rank is but the guinea's stamp,
The Man's the gowd for a' that.

What though on hamely fare we dine,
Wear hoddin grey, an' a that;
Gie fools their silks, and knaves their wine;
A Man's a Man for a' that:
For a' that, and a' that,
Their tinsel show, an' a' that;
The honest man, tho' e'er sae poor,
Is king o' men for a' that.

A prince can mak a belted knight,
A marquis, duke, an' a' that;
But an honest man's abon his might,
Gude faith, he maunna fa' that!
For a' that, an' a' that,
Their dignities an' a' that;
The pith o' sense, an' pride o' worth,

Are higher rank than a' that.

Then let us pray that come it may,
(As come it will for a' that,)
That Sense and Worth, o'er a' the earth,
Shall bear the gree, an' a' that.
For a' that, an' a' that,
It's coming yet for a' that,
That Man to Man, the world o'er,
Shall brothers be for a' that.

NARRATOR: In 1789 Robert's brother William, eight years younger than Robert, died. Robert had looked after him after their father departed this life. William had lacked ambition and a good start in life, but Burns helped him into the saddlery business with an apprenticeship in Edinburgh, Carlisle, and then Newcastle. Once trained, he moved as a time-served saddler to London.

An exchange of letters gives an indication of events:

WILLIAM: "Dear Sir. Longtown, February 15th, 1789.

As I am now in a manner only entering into the world, I begin this our correspondence, with a view of being a gainer by your advice.

I now stand on my own bottom. I am very conscious of being called to act in life whether I will or not, and my inexperience which I daily feel makes me wish for that advice which you are so able to give and which I can only expect from you or Gilbert since the loss of the kindest and ablest of fathers.

I left Dumfries about five o'clock and came to Annan to breakfast and staid about an hour, and I reached this place about two o'clock. I have got work here and I intend to stay a month or six weeks and then go forward as I wish to be at York about the latter end of summer, where I propose to spend next winter and go on for London in the spring.

Please send me, the first Wednesday after you receive this, by the Carlisle wagon two of my coarse shirts, one of my best linen ones, my velveteen vest, and a neck cloth. Write to me along with them and direct to my Saddler, in Longtown.

Believe me to be your affectionate and obliged brother, William Burns.

P.S. The greatcoat you gave me at parting did me singular service the day I come here."

BURNS: "My Dear Willliam. Ellisland, 5th May, 1789.

I am happy to hear by yours from Newcastle that you are getting some employ.

I had a visit of your old friend and landlord. In the midst of a drunken frolic in Dumfries, he took it into his head to come and see me; and I took all the pains in my power to please and entertain the old veteran. He is high in your praises and I would advise you to cultivate his friendship, as he is in his way a worthy and to you may be a useful man.

Anderson, I hope will have your shoes ready to send by the wagon tomorrow. I forgot to mention the circumstance of making them pumps.

Your falling in love is indeed a phenomenon. To a fellow of your turn it cannot be hurtful. I am you know a veteran in these campaigns, so let me advise you always to pay your particular assiduities and try for intimacy as soon as you feel the first symptoms of the passion.

I shall be in Ayrshire about a fortnight. Your sisters send their compliments. God Bless You.
Robert Burns."

WILLIAM: "Newcastle, 24th January, 1790.

Dear Brother, I wrote to you about six weeks ago, and have expected to hear from you every post since, but I suppose your excise business which you hinted at in your last has prevented you from writing.

I intend to sail for London in a fortnight or three weeks at farthest. You promised to write me some instructions about behaviour in companies rather above my station. I wish you could write me such instructions now; I never had more need of them, for having spent little of my time in company of any sort since I came to Newcastle, I have almost forgot the common civilities of life.

I am, & etc. W.B."

NARRATOR: And sad news and a sympathetic letter from John Murdoch to Burns.

MURDOCH: "Hart-Street, Bloomsberry Square, London. September 14th, 1790.

My Dear Friend. Yours of the 16th July, I received on the 26th per favour of my friend Mr Kennedy, and was informed at the same time that your brother was ill. I set out next morning to see him but, when I went to Mr Barber's, to my great astonishment and heartfelt grief I found my young friend, William, had, on Saturday, bid an everlasting farewell to sublunary things.

Be assured, my dear friend, that I cordially sympathise with you all and particularly with Mrs Burns, who is undoubtedly one of the most tender and affectionate mothers that ever lived. Remember me to her in the most friendly manner when you see her.

Please present my best compliments to Mrs R. Burns, and to your brothers and sisters.

One of the most pleasing hopes I have is to visit you all; but I am commonly disappointed in what I most ardently wish for.

I am Dear Sir, Yours sincerely, John Murdoch."

NARRATOR: Robert was occasionally in trouble for his anti-Government comments.

There was one incident which landed him in serious trouble with his employers: as a Volunteer, he and others boarded the smuggling brig *Rosamund* and, as a trophy, Burns purchased four carronades which he immediately sent to the French Convention with a letter expressing admiration! The guns and letter were intercepted at the English Channel. After a full-scale investigation he was told to "act, don't think, be silent, and obey". Sadly, he had to accept the criticism, but was in no position to argue his natural sympathies.

Another edition of his work was published by Creech in 1793.

SONG: "THE BANKS O' DOON"

Sweet are the banks – the banks o' Doon,
The spreading flowers are fair,
And everything is blythe and glad,
But I am fu' o' care.
Thou'll break my heart, thou bonie bird,
That sings upon the bough;
Thou minds me o' the happy days
When my fause Luve was true:
Thou'll break my heart, thou bonie bird,
That sings beside thy mate;
For sae I sat, and sae I sang,
And wist na o' my fate.

Aft hae I rov'd by bonie Doon,
To see the woodbine twine;
And ilka birds sang o' its Luve,

And sae did I o' mine:
Wi' lightsome heart I pu'd a rose,
Upon its thorny tree;
But my fause Luver staw my rose
And left the thorn wi' me:
Wi' lightsome heart I pu'd a rose,
Upon a morn in June;
And sae I flourished on the morn,
And sae was pu'd or noon!

NARRATOR: Robbie's humour, which has been referred to previously, was always evident in his work. Here again are two examples of his satire. There were two local ladies – a Miss Duncan, who was of small and lean proportions, and a Mrs Arbuckle, who was much larger than plump. Burns was asked by an acquaintance why God had made Miss D. so little and Mrs A. so big. His reply came in one four-line verse.

VERSE "ON BEING ASKED WHY GOD MADE MISS D SO LITTLE AND MRS A SO BIG"

Ask why God made the GEM so small,
And why so huge the granite?
Because God meant, mankind should set
That higher value on it.

NARRATOR: And in one eight-line verse, he responds satirically to the question of marriage:

VERSE: "MARRIAGE"

That hackney'd judge of human life,
The Preacher and the King,
Observes: "The man that gets a wife
He gets a noble thing."
But how capricious are mankind,
Now loathing, now desirous!
We married men, how oft we find
The best of things will tire us!

NARRATOR: Burns then completed the two great collections of songs for James Johnson and for some time remained active, very creative and mentally alert. However, in the summer of 1794 his health began to decline. He wrote to Mrs Dunlop about the ill-thought actions of his youth. Medical friends warned him of "flying gout".

His doctors assessed him as having a severe heart condition, and he was relieved to be informed that his decline was not related to drink or to women but to a genetic condition.

In September 1795 he lost his only daughter, Elizabeth. Later that year he suffered a debilitating fever and said, in a letter to a friend, "this has brought me to the borders of the grave".

His general health was rapidly deteriorating. His finances were in a bad state, thus requiring him to seek an advance of one guinea from his employers. His colleagues, aware of his distress, did his job as well as their own, and passed the earnings over to Robert. With no clear medical advice he felt that the summer weather would provide some relief. Jean was expecting a baby, and a friend was brought in to nurse him.

BURNS: I was getting weaker by the day. My sole concern was for my family after I'd gone. I wrote farewell letters to friends, and was forced to beg for money from my family in Montrose. I had to write to Mr Armour asking if his wife could come to help Jean. To cap it all, the authorities were chasing me for money for my Volunteer uniform.

At the end of June, I went to Brow on the Solway Firth; sea-bathing had been recommended. Initially I felt better, and I returned to Dumfries on the 18th of July. How I made that journey I'll never know – even worse, I had to climb the stairs to my bedroom.

My dear wife was in need of help. I had to write to her father, James Armour:

"My Dear Sir. Dumfries, 18th July, 1796.

Do, for heaven's sake, send Mrs Armour here immediately. My wife is hourly expecting to be put to bed. Good God! What a situation for her to be in, poor girl, without a friend. I returned from sea-bathing quarters today, and my medical friends would almost persuade me that I am better, but I think and feel that my strength is so gone that the disorder will prove fatal to me.

Your son-in-law, R.B."

I had done what I could to find help. My senses told me I was finished. All I could do was wait for the end. What dominated my thoughts was the obvious financial insecurity of my family. My life, I reflected, seemed to be all about my melancholy, money problems and farming bad luck, but – as Gilbert had said all those years ago – the one word that summed me up was passion, and I could not deny that all of my life had been passionate. Was it the case that, after all, my life was – it seemed – all about poetry and bad luck? Oh, and yes: my weaknesses?

Yes; perhaps I was that dazzling meteor that faded away.

Burns lies down on a bed or couch.

NARRATOR: It could be said Robert Burns' bad luck was summarised by those last few days at the Solway, when he believed he was – on good advice – taking sea-bathing as a remedy, when in fact it was the most damaging thing he could have done.
Robert died on the morning of Thursday 21st July 1796, in his 38th year.

At this point Burns should be covered by a white sheet.

NARRATOR: Robert Burns, born a genius, was unlucky in health and wealth. Had he been a successful farmer, emigrated to Jamaica or walked off with Clarinda, we would not likely have seen his prolific works. His mother Agnes kindled a flame in Robbie, and he magnified that bright light for us by his writings which have stretched around the world because of his love for his fellow man.

Robert's body lay in the house as silent crowds paid their last respects.

At this point, all the cast, except the Narrator, file past Burns – males removing hats and bowing heads.

NARRATOR: His body was moved on Saturday 23rd to Dumfries Town Hall for a service, and he was interred in the north-east corner of St Michael's cemetery.

Scotland quickly concluded a genius had gone. We are left with the question: why was his mighty influence with his pen not realised long before he passed away? A man of such literary stature indeed deserved greater recognition, and a more fitting end.

No-one could have guessed that when his parents travelled from Dunnotter to Ayrshire that the unique combination of parents, teacher, environment and a clever child would produce a literary giant. What more could his enlightened father have asked for?

We could say that the gale force wind which so nearly carried him, as an infant, away from us was in fact notice being served that a "wind of change" was coming.

Can you imagine a Scotland if Burns had never lived? And what would he make of things today?

SONG: "AULD LANG SYNE"

[The guests, led by the cast.]

Should auld acquaintance be forgot,
And never brought to mind?
Should auld acquaintance be forgot,
And auld lang syne!

For auld lang syne, my jo,
For auld lang syne,
We'll tak a cup o' kindness yet,
For auld lang syne.

And surely ye'll be your pint stowp!
And surely I'll be mine!
And we'll take a cup o' kindness yet,
For auld lang syne.

We twa hae run about the braes,
And pou'd the gowan fine;
But we've wander'd mony a weary fitt,
Sin' auld lang syne.

We twa hae paidl'd in the burn,

Frae morning sun till dine;
But seas between us braid hae roar'd
Sin' auld lang syne.

And there's a hand, my trusty fiere!
And gie's a hand o' thine!
And we'll tak a right gude-willie-waught,
For auld lang syne.

For auld lang syne, my jo,
For auld lang syne,
We'll tak a cup o' kindness yet,
For auld lang syne.

Appendix I
Address to a Haggis

Fair fa'[2] your honest sonsie[3] face
Great Chieftain o' the Puddin-race!
Aboon[4] them a' ye tak your place,
Painch,[5] tripe, or thairm:
Weel are ye wordy[6] o' a grace
As lang's my arm.

The groaning trencher there ye fill,
Your hurdies[7] like a distant hill,
Your pin wad help to mend a mill
In time o' need,
While thro' your pores the dews distil
Like amber bead.

His knife see Rustic-labour dight,[8]
An' cut you up wi' ready sleight,
Trenching your gushing entrails bright
Like onie[9] ditch;

---

[2] Good luck
[3] Jolly
[4] Above
[5] Intestines
[6] Worthy
[7] Buttocks
[8] Wipe

And then, O what a glorious sight,
Warm-reekin,[10] rich!

Then, horn for horn they stretch an' strive[11]
Deil tak the hindmost, on they drive,
Till a' their weel-swall'd kytes[12] believe
Are bent like drums;
Then auld Guidman, maist like to rive,[13]
'Bethankit'[14] hums.

Is there that owre[15] his French ragout,
Or olio that wad staw[16] a sow,
O fricassee wad mak her spew
Wi' perfect sconner,
Looks down wi 'sneering, scornful view
On sic a dinner?

Poor devil see him ower his trash,
As feckless as a wither'd rash,[17]
His spindle shank[18] a guid whip-lash,

---

[9] Any
[10] Steaming
[11] Spoon
[12] Swelled stomachs
[13] Burst
[14] 'God be Thanked'
[15] Over
[16] Would surfeit
[17] Rush
[18] Thin

His nieve[19] a nit;
Thro' bluidy flood or field to dash,
O how unfit!

But mark the Rustic, haggis-fed,
The trembling earth resounds his tread;
Clapin his walie nieve[20] a blade,
He'll mak it whissle;
An' legs an' arms, an' heads will send
Like taps o' thrissle.[21]

Ye Pow'rs wha mak mankind your care
And dish them out their bill o' fare,
Auld Scotland wants nae skinking ware[22]
That jaups in luggies;[23]
But if ye wish her gratefu' prayer,
Gie[24] her a Haggis!

---

[19] Closed fist
[20] Large fist
[21] Tops of thistles
[22] Thin stuff
[23] Splashes in bowls
[24] Give

Appendix II
The Selkirk Grace

Some hae meat and canna eat
And some wad eat that want it:
But we hae meat and we can eat,
And sae the Lord be thankit.

Appendix III
A Typical Burns Night Menu

Haggis, Neeps,[25] and Tatties[26]

* * *

Lentil Soup and Crusty Roll

* * *

Steak Pie
or
Chicken and Oatmeal Stuffing

* * *

Apple Pie and Ice Cream
or
Cheese and Oatcakes

* * *

Coffee and Mints

---

[25] 'Neeps' are turnips.
[26] The term 'Tatties' refers to potatoes.

Appendix IV
The Loyal Toast

Ladies and Gentlemen, I ask you to be upstanding to toast our Sovereign Queen – Elizabeth.

The Queen.

Appendix V
The Immortal Memory (Example)

Mr Chairman, Honoured Guests, Ladies and Gentlemen:
    I am doubly honoured to stand here this evening. Well I'm amazed, Mr Chairman, after such a delicious feast and generous drinks, that I'm able to stand after your very kind hospitality for which I thank you.
    First, to share this unique evening with you all, and second, to have this opportunity to honour and pay tribute to my hero, your hero and OUR hero: Robert, Rabbie, Robbie or Robin Burns.
    Now, we all know Robert Burns was a Lowlander and that ordinary Highland dress such as the plaid or kilt was not part of his culture. Not his dress code.
    I have wrestled for years with the problem of associating Burns with tartan, but in preparing for this evening I have at long last found a rationale at least I think I have, because following the Culloden disaster, Clan Chiefs were removed and any form of garment woven like a tartan was banned by the Dress Act of 1746. That Act was repealed in 1782.
    And here's my rationale: for Rabbie, it would have been a symbol of defiance for Scotland to regain its right from a British government of 1782 to wear tartan. So that's it – Burns and tartan do go together. That's the reason why I'm wearing so much tartan this evening.

In 1757, William Burns (or Burness) and his wife Agnes were on their way from Kincardineshire to a new life in Ayrshire. Little could they ever imagine that well over 260 years later, people would – on the anniversary of the birth of their firstborn – gather round in meetings not just in wee Scottish towns and villages, but in almost every part of the world to acclaim the life and works of their yet-unborn child. Someone who was to be hailed as a writer greater even than Shakespeare, Longfellow or Joyce.

And how did we come to be so blessed with the genius of a man from humble farming stock?

We must first thank his caring mother, who sparked Robbie's mind with old tales and ghostly stories, followed by the earnest desire of his father to educate his sons. Then the dedication of a thoughtful and influential teacher of classics and language – none other than John Murdoch.

Despite his father's efforts, Robbie Burns did not have it easy: he was left to farm poor land, to be saddled with debt, and to work long hours through the night on his poetry. The high demands he put on himself to write, and his financial worries, created regular bouts of depression (or melancholy as he called it) which he suffered. Hard and exhausting work accompanied him throughout his life – right up to the end. Today, he may have had medication to help. In his day, and in his way, he found relaxation with the lasses – but as we know, those pursuits did not always go so well either.

However, there may be another, more fundamental reason for us to find Robert Burns – the climate. Did his father merely wish to get away from the miserable cold and inhospitable coastline of the North Sea, and by chance find a world which was full of stimulus for a writer – complete with John Murdoch? Robbie was produced obviously by his intellect, but also by chance.

Where does one start to say something about Robert Burns? It's not a case of what facts one must seek out about this wonderful and remarkable man, but rather what information must be discarded because time, this evening, does not permit. It's best perhaps to examine what he wrote about his aims in life:

"Yes, I may have had weaknesses, but I was passionate about many things – my ardent desire to learn and read and to study great writers, and my strong wish to learn about my fellow man – especially the poor in society. I discovered satire and humour to expose and lampoon vanity, arrogance and hypocrisy whenever I witnessed it. My deep inner conviction was to be a voice in Scotland, to make a mark as a writer."

As a young teenager he also wrote:

"I want to be a poet and an ambassador in my own land."

On the subject of passion, he happily once said:

"Yes, when I loved a lass – it was always passionate. But my public confessions were equally passionate."

He also said: "I grew up in the countryside. I wrote about my roots and everything around me. I took time to study, and was fascinated by the beauty of Mother Nature."

Robert's environment made him what he was. Despite the poverty and hard work he experienced, Robbie Burns tried to make all the right decisions about his farms and his publications. But in his own words, he once said: "When you are a dreamer, a romantic and writer, it's difficult to keep your feet on the ground."

He added: "I discovered I had a very deep romantic side to me. When I loved – I loved."

Let's look at all the "ifs" in his life that gave us the great man we know:

IF his caring mum hadn't ignited a furnace in young Robert's mind with her old tales and stories of ghosts and ghouls.

IF his insightful father hadn't prized education so highly for his son.

IF John Murdoch hadn't been around to teach him classics, French, Latin and philosophy.

IF the farms at Mount Oliphant, Tarbolton and Mossgeil had been more fertile and the harvests more favourable and profitable, he may have settled for a less demanding life with his pen.

IF Mary Campbell had not tragically died of a fever in Greenock while waiting to be joined by Robert, they would have set sail for the West Indies.

IF Mary McLehose (AKA "Clarinda", Robbie's secret friend) had been prepared to leave her husband, Robert may have set off in a totally different direction. Luckily for us, "Ae Fond Kiss" was all they enjoyed.

Yes, many IFs – and there's too many to mention now. But you know I maintain, the problems he endured did not dim him – they made him.

I would like to add that Robert has been put down by some distinguished writers as a womaniser and a rogue. But the long list of ladies or lasses was not as ruinous as it may seem. Yes, he was rebuked by the Kirk, but no one (except for Jean Armour's father) ever said a bad word about him. He loved and he was loved. He suffered, as many geniuses do, from sitting on that knife edge of brilliance and despair. He suffered those many bouts of melancholy. My submission is that the lassies in his life saved him by providing emotional support. He was a highly sensitive man. What's wrong with needing a shoulder to cry on – especially a bonnie lassie's shoulder? His harsh life and mental stress did not hinder him; it made him. He was resilient.

On 13th January 1787, while he was in Edinburgh being acclaimed for his literary success, the Grand Master Mason of Scotland proposed a toast in honour of Robert: "To Caledonia and Caledonia's Bard – Brother Burns". Robert was the main attraction in the city. He had arrived on a borrowed pony, and left knowing many high-ranking friends and acquaintances in the most eminent disciplines in the capital. Yes, that was our Robbie.

There's not a huge amount written about his physical appearance, but when in Edinburgh the 16-year-old Walter Scott was in the audience and listened to Burns at a gathering. The most telling description I like to relate is that Scott later recalled – and I quote – "I found

Robert Burns to be a strong robust figure with a dignified plainness. He was a man of strong expression. His eyes glowed when he spoke with feeling or interest. I never saw such an eye in a human head. In conversation he was confident without presumption, and amongst the top men of his time he expressed himself with firmness and modesty."

How about that for a description of our great man? No wonder the lassies fell at his feet – and can you blame them?

This man today would have been a captivating, charismatic TV personality. An actor, perhaps? A must for every TV show. A must when the TV producer wanted a plain man to present "the people's ideas and problems". He would have been a heart throb. He would have been a journalist's dream: erudite, brilliant, with a lot of juicy background material to whet the appetite. The paparazzi would have gone wild with delight. There would have been queues miles long to sign him up as an after-dinner speaker.

And yet Robert Burns was forever self-analytical. When he found himself the centre of attraction – feted in Edinburgh, with honours heaped upon him – he was quick to caution himself. At the time, he said, "I am only too well aware of being a meteor – aye, quick to burst into dazzling brilliance, but equally quick to fade away". This was the realist; the unassuming Robbie.

And when he lay on his deathbed in Dumfries in July 1796 at the age of 37, he recalled his own words when he was at his highest point in Edinburgh and wrote: "Am I that dazzling meteor after all – the one that faded away?"

And so, Robert Burns: you were not a dazzling meteor that dimmed. You are brighter today than you could ever have imagined. We need you here. Come back and give us your genius.

We would be inspired to hear your take on our lives on our mortal coil here today. If only you were with us to give us a line or two (satirical, critical or humorous) about topical issues.

Robbie, you sometimes wrote about the despair of your people in your day. We could do with a good portion of your wit about the despair we sometimes have to live with today.

We toast your brilliance:

Your love for your fellow man,

Your genius in finding a way in your writings of presenting the plight of your fellow citizens of your day.

You certainly did find a way of getting your Kilmarnock Edition "in guid black print" as you dreamed.

And can I say that your writings today are in better and blacker ink than you ever imagined. Aye, and in some languages that would have amused you.

Thank you, Robert Burns, for your legacy. We promise to keep it alive. You have left us a rich heritage, and we hold your memory dear.

Finally, my friends, a wee story.

Robert and his brother Gilbert were watching the hens and the cockerel clucking their way around the farmyard. They watched as the cockerel took a very close interest in some hens and then obviously prepared to show one of them his stuff, when the farmer's wife came out and scattered some seed. Immediately, all the birds – including the cockerel – ran to peck what they could get.

Robert turned to Gilbert and said, "Gilbert, I hope I'll never be as hungry as that cockerel".

Immortal is undying, immortal is deathless, exempt from death and decay. Never has there been a truer word or description about Robert Burns. Raconteur, wit, writer, poet, farmer, exciseman, soldier – you make us proud to be Scots.

This is an unforgettable evening for me, Mr Chairman, because of the honour you have bestowed upon me, and I thank you all for listening.

As a Scot, it gives me huge pleasure to propose a toast to the greatest Scot who ever lived. I ask you all, whatever your native heath, to fill your glasses to overflowing.

Let me preface the toast with the words Robert himself first heard in Edinburgh in 1787. Let us bring that toast to life again, this evening, here in —.

Mr Chairman, distinguished guests, ladies and gentlemen. I ask you to be upstanding and raise your glasses high as I give you the toast of a man whose life was short but memory of him immortal.

The toast is to:

"Caledonia and Caledonia's Bard: the Immortal ROBERT BURNS."

Appendix VI
Toast to the Lassies (Example)

How wonderful to see so many bonnie lassies here this evening – and so well turned out, all with special hairdos and a touch of lipstick too! But you don't need that – you're all bonny as you are!

Most of all, it's just great to see your smiling faces.

I am certain, gentlemen, that in the privacy of our domestic bliss we express our love, devotion and gratitude for the contribution our lasses make to our daily lives.

Over the years there have been many 'male only' Burns suppers, but frankly I don't know why it took so long to invite the fairer sex. I'm certain Robbie himself would have welcomed the ladies.

Aye, the Tarbolton Bachelors enjoyed their evenings, but I'm certain an evening with the lassies was not far from their minds.

Now, I know there are some – if not many – in history (and even today!) who may have held doubtful views about the Bard and his lassies. Some may even suggest he treated them badly. But it's simply not true. He never mistreated or intentionally damaged a lassie. Well, a bairn's no damage – for remember, it "taks twa tae tango!"

Nobody had a bad word to say about Robbie. Well, admittedly, maybe Jean Armour's father did for a while. And remember, he was betrothed to Mary Campbell and would have gone to the West Indies with her. He didn't evade his responsibilities.

Rabbie had his lasses. There was his first girlfriend, Nellie Kirkpatrick, and Peggy Thomson, then Elizabeth Paton – yes, and a few others. But his real love was his long-lasting love: Jean.

We must remember, our Robbie was a genius. He was a sensitive man, in tune with life, love, Mother Nature, and the world around him. Like many highly talented people, he suffered in silence with loneliness, doubts and fears. He called it his "melancholy". Today it may be labelled stress or depression. He needed comfort, companionship and understanding. Without the lassies in his life, we may never have heard brilliant works. We owe it to the ladies.

As Rabbie himself said, "Aye, I was always passionate – but my confessions from the cutty stool were passionate too!"

Robbie was an intellectual giant, a wit, a charmer. And while we boys here may not have these qualities (well, there are a few charmers around), we need the lassies every bit as much as Robbie did. If we had Robbie's talents, we would write poems and songs about the lass in our life too.

You help us, support us and you love us and, aye, we need you – in every way!

So, as Robert Burns would say, "Have a drink and celebrate the lassies". So gentlemen, will you please be upstanding, raise your glasses, and join me in a toast:

"To the Lassies."

* * *

SHORT VERSION

Lassies were an important part in the life and work of Robert Burns – as indeed, gentlemen, they are in ours. We acknowledge on this special evening all their help, not only by their attendance here but their contribution to our wellbeing throughout the year. We compliment you on looking, as always, so wonderful for us. Gentlemen, I ask you to rise and toast the Lassies: what would life be like without them?

"The Lassies."

Appendix VII
Reply from the Lassies (Example)

Thank you for your kind words Mr —. I'm sure you deliver them from the heart. I am delighted to respond on behalf of the Lassies. We thank you for your kind remarks of appreciation, and we are flattered by your compliments which I'm certain we all graciously accept.

If we could speak to Rabbie's lassies today, I'm sure they would say: "Aye, you would do the same for your man". Yes, as you say, Robbie was a giant in literature – but he was also a captivating figure, and we honour him as much as you do.

He was a charming man and, if he were with us today, he would be mobbed wherever he went – interviewed on TV, with journalists hanging on to his every word. Yes, the lassies would be falling at his feet.

But it's no different today. When you work late or enjoy a drink at the pub, we understand your pressures. And of course, we comfort you when you suffer your own melancholy when your football or rugby team is defeated or you have frustrations at work. We acknowledge your help in the household, even if we show you how to do things right.

We know that you love us and that we need you to hammer in a nail, to weed the garden, keep the car clean and check the bank balance. We may complain about you needing a haircut or walking in with dirty feet on our clean floor, or the need to gently prompt you about a birthday or anniversary card. But underneath all of that, we need you and love you.

So, lads, gents, husbands, boyfriends: we thank you for your kind words. We'll look after you, for I know you look after us. We need you and your credit card, and we couldn't live without you.

It is indeed a pleasure that the days of the old "boys only" Burns' suppers are nearly over, and we can join you to have such complimentary tributes paid to us.

Ladies, it is my privilege on your behalf that – having had a good-humoured and loving dig at our other halves – I ask you to rise and please join me in toasting our bonnie laddies:

"To the Laddies."

* * *

SHORT VERSION

Thank you, Mr —, for those kind words. I am delighted to respond on behalf of the Lassies. We thank you for your kind remarks of appreciation, and we are flattered by your compliments which we graciously accept. Ladies, it is my pleasure to ask you to rise and toast the "The Laddies" – how can we exist without them?

"To the Laddies."

Appendix VIII
Auld Lang Syne

Should auld acquaintance be forgot,
And never brought to mind?
Should auld acquaintance be forgot,
And auld lang syne!

For auld lang syne, my jo,
For auld lang syne,
We'll tak a cup o' kindness yet,
For auld lang syne.

And surely ye'll be your pint stowp!
And surely I'll be mine!
And we'll take a cup o' kindness yet,
For auld lang syne.

We twa hae run about the braes,
And pou'd the gowan fine;
But we've wander'd mony a weary fitt,
Sin' auld lang syne.

We twa hae paidl'd in the burn,
Frae morning sun till dine;
But seas between us braid hae roar'd
Sin' auld lang syne.

And there's a hand, my trusty fiere!
And gie's a hand o' thine!
And we'll tak a right gude-willie-waught,
For auld lang syne.

For auld lang syne, my jo,
For auld lang syne,
We'll tak a cup o' kindness yet,
For auld lang syne.

Illustrations

Robert Burns

As portrayed by Robert Murray

Narrator #1

As portrayed by Joy Taylor

Narrator #2

As portrayed by Michael Rae

Reader

As portrayed by Sheila Brunton

Singer

As portrayed by Patricia Rae

Alison Begbie

As portrayed by Patricia Evans

The Rev. Dr Hugh Blair
As portrayed by Brian McCartney

Gilbert Burns

As portrayed by Howard Evans

Clarinda

As portrayed by Gillian Dissel

Jean Armour and Scamp

As portrayed by Eleanor Jewson and Phoenix

John Murdoch

As portrayed by Steven Swann

William Burns

As portrayed by Rodger Brunton

Acknowledgements

To Ian McDougall.

To Louise Burness.

To Mr Duguid of the Burns Federation for authentic letters.

To Mr John Blair for the short version speeches.

To Rodger Brunton for making Comrie Hall available for the first stage presentation.

To James Hutcheson and his cast for the first and successive productions.

To all of my friends whose photos appear in the Illustrations section, who took part in the play in Hamish and Fiona's home.

To James 'Peem' Murray for the photography.

About the Author

Robert Taylor Murray was born in Barry, near Carnoustie, in 1940. Growing up in Westhaven and later residing in Carnoustie itself, he attended Barry and Carnoustie Schools before becoming an apprentice grocer with William Low & Company Ltd. He qualified as a Member of The Grocers' Institute, and was appointed manager of William Low's Brantwood branch in Dundee, becoming the company's youngest ever manager at the age of 19. He later oversaw the Logie Street branch in Lochee.

Robert went on to manage a larger third branch in Dundee and then, after attending further education management courses, discovered he was sufficiently qualified to successfully apply for a post as a lecturer in distributive trades subjects at Dundee Commercial College – a position he held for five years. Realising how much the retail trade was changing and feeling he was less in touch to reflect the current scene, he applied to join The Grocers' Institute and was appointed Training Development Officer for part of London and east England, where he advised companies and colleges on training in the retail grocery trade.

After two years he returned to the Dundee area when he was appointed Training Officer for Watson & Philip, a national wholesale food distributor. He remained with that company for thirty-three years, during which time he was appointed Personnel Manager and eventually became Group Personnel Manager with responsibility for three thousand employees and, latterly, in the London area.

Following a company acquisition he became redundant at the age of sixty-two. In retirement he has again been actively involved in amateur theatre. He is a member of Tay Writers – a Dundee based writing group – and Angus Writers' Circle, and writes short stories.

Robert's autobiographical account of his early days in retail, *The Grocer's Boy*, was published by Extremis Publishing in 2018. His stage presentation on the life of Robert Burns, *The Spirit of Robbie Burns*, has been performed several times around the country.

He has two daughters, each married, and four grandchildren. When he is not writing, he enjoys travelling, hill walking and golfing.

Also Available from Extremis Publishing

The Grocer's Boy
A Slice of His Life in 1950s Scotland

By Robert Murray

The 1950s in Carnoustie: a beautiful seaside town on the Tayside coast, and a place which was to see rapid social and technological advancement during one of the fastest-moving periods of cultural change in recent British history.

In *The Grocer's Boy*, Robert Murray relates his account of an eventful childhood in post-War Scotland, drawing on fond memories of his loving family, his droll and often mischievous group of friends, and the many inspirational people who influenced him and helped to shape his early life.

Join Robert on his adventures in retail as he advances from his humble beginnings as a delivery boy for the famous William Low grocery firm, all the way to becoming the youngest manager in the company's history at just nineteen years of age. Read tales of his hectic, hard-working time as an apprentice grocer — sometimes humorous, occasionally nerve-wracking, but never less than entertaining.

From Robert's early romances and passion for stage performance to his long-running battle of wits with his temperamental delivery bike, *The Grocer's Boy* is a story of charm and nostalgia; the celebration of a happy youth in a distinctive bygone age.

Also Available from Extremis Publishing

Exploring the NC500

Travelling Scotland's Route 66

By David M. Addison

Travelling anti-clockwise, David M. Addison seeks his kicks on Scotland's equivalent of Route 66. Otherwise known as NC500, the route takes you through five hundred miles of some of Scotland's most spectacular scenery. No wonder it has been voted as one of the world's five most scenic road journeys.

There are many ways of exploring the NC500. You can drive it, cycle it, motorbike it or even walk it, even if you are not one of The Proclaimers! And there are as many activities, places of interest and sights to be seen along the way as there are miles.

This is a personal account of the author's exploration of the NC500 as well as some detours from it, such as to the Black Isle, Strathpeffer and Dingwall. Whatever your reason or reasons for exploring the NC500 may be, you should read this book before you go, or take it with you as a *vade mecum*. It will enhance your appreciation of the NC500 as you learn about the history behind the turbulent past of the many castles; hear folk tales, myths and legends connected with the area; become acquainted with the ancient peoples who once lived in this timeless landscape, and read about the lives of more recent heroes such as the good Hugh Miller who met a tragic end and villains such as the notorious Duke of Sutherland, who died in his bed (and may not be quite as bad as he is painted). There are a good number of other characters too of whom you may have never heard: some colourful, some eccentric, some *very* eccentric.

You may not necessarily wish to follow in the author's footsteps in all that he did, but if you read this book you will certainly see the landscape through more informed eyes as you do whatever you want to do *en route* NC500.

Sit in your car and enjoy the scenery for its own sake (and remember you get a different perspective from a different direction, so you may want to come back and do it again to get an alternative point of view!), or get out and explore it at closer quarters – the choice is yours, but this book will complement your experience, whatever you decide.

Also Available from Extremis Publishing

Victories at Sea
In Films and TV

By Colin M. Barron

Naval battles have inspired countless films and television dramas over the years, recounting the bravery and tragedy that have unfolded over centuries of conflict on the high seas.

Victories at Sea considers the many different aspects of warfare on (and below) the waves as they have been depicted on screen, discussing such topics as amphibious operations, carrier warfare, underwater sabotage, and Cold War strategies. Covering films ranging from vintage World War II classics to modern seaborne thrillers, the book investigates the real-life stories which lay behind the production of these features as well as how they eventually came to be received at the box-office.

From blockbuster Hollywood epics to must-see television series, *Victories at Sea* is a comprehensive guide to the greats of the genre, combining a forensic eye for detail with meticulous analysis of the features under discussion. With discussion of low-budget dramas and high-octane action movies alike, this examination of naval warfare on the big and small screens relates all of the exhilaration and gallantry that have made these films such lasting favourites amongst cinema and TV aficionados.

Also Available from Extremis Publishing

Contested Mindscapes
Exploring Approaches to Dementia in Modern Popular Culture

By Thomas A. Christie

Dementia is a mental health condition which affects an estimated 50 million people worldwide. Yet it has, until recently, been an unfairly neglected subject in popular culture.

Contested Mindscapes considers the ways in which the arts have engaged with dementia over the past twenty years, looking at particular examples drawn from the disciplines of film and television, popular music, performance art, and interactive entertainment.

Examining a variety of creative approaches ranging from the thought-provoking to the controversial, *Contested Mindscapes* carefully contemplates the many ways in which the humanities and entertainment industries have engaged with dementia, exploring how the wide-ranging implications of this complex condition have been communicated through a variety of artistic nodes.

Also Available from Extremis Publishing

The Fearn Bobby
Reflections from a Life in Scottish Policing
By Ian McNeish

'It's all about the community', the words of Kenneth Ross, Chief Constable of Ross and Sutherland Constabulary, guided Ian McNeish through thirty years of police service. They were true then, back in 1974, and they are true now.

Ian held a police warrant card for three decades, serving communities across Scotland. In that time, his work saw him moving from the northerly constabulary where he policed the rural Hill of Fearn to the social challenges that presented themselves amongst the urban landscape of Central Scotland.

From his formative years in post-War Scotland through to his application to join the police service, Ian has led a rich and varied professional life that ranged from working in iron foundries to building electronic parts for the Kestrel Jump Jet and legendary Concorde aircraft. But once he had joined the police service, he found himself faced with a whole new range of life-changing experiences – some of them surprising, a few even shocking, but all of them memorable.

Leading the reader through his involvement in front line situations, Ian explains the effects of anti-social behaviour and attending criminal court appearances, in addition to dealing with death and the responsibilities of informing those left behind. He considers topics such as ethics, public interest, police and firearms, drug issues, causes of crime, and a lot more besides.

In a career where his duties ranged from policing national strikes to providing comfort and support through personal tragedies, Ian advanced through the ranks and saw first-hand the vital importance of effective management and good teamwork. Whether as the 'Fearn Bobby', policing a remote countryside outpost, as a seconded officer working for the Chief Executive of a Regional Council, or as a Local Unit Commander in Bo'ness, Ian always knew the importance of putting the community first. Comparing today's policing techniques with his own professional experiences and examining both the good times and the harrowing pitfalls of the job, his account of life in the force is heartfelt, entertaining, and always completely honest.

Also Available from Extremis Publishing

Tales from the Western Front

By Ed Dixon

Tales from the Western Front is a collection of stories about the people and places encountered by the author during more than three decades of visiting the battlefields, graveyards, towns and villages of France and Belgium.

Characters tragic and comic, famous and humble live within these pages, each connected by the common thread of the Great War. Meet Harry Lauder, the great Scottish entertainer and first international superstar; Tommy Armour, golf champion and war hero; "Hoodoo" Kinross, VC, the Pride of Lougheed; the Winslow Boy; Albert Ball, and Jackie the Soldier Baboon among many others.

Each chapter is a story in itself and fully illustrated with photos past and present.

For details of new and forthcoming books
from Extremis Publishing,
please visit our official website at:

www.extremispublishing.com

or follow us on social media at:

www.facebook.com/extremispublishing

www.linkedin.com/company/extremis-publishing-ltd-/

www.ingramcontent.com/pod-product-compliance
Lightning Source LLC
Chambersburg PA
CBHW070607010526
44118CB00012B/1463